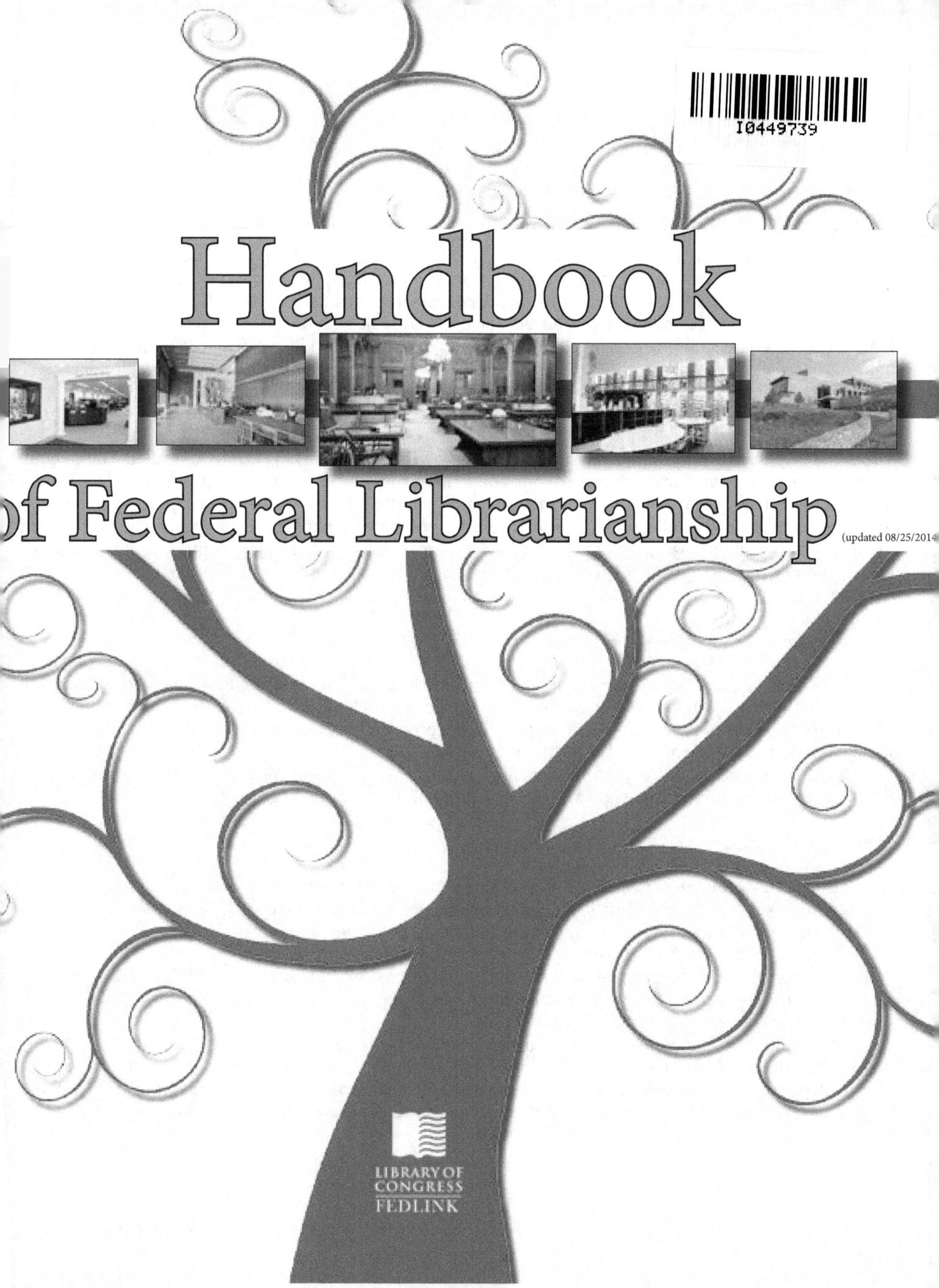

Handbook

of Federal Librarianship

(updated 08/25/2014)

LIBRARY OF
CONGRESS
FEDLINK

Preface

The Handbook of Federal Librarianship is a project of the Federal Library and Information Network's (FEDLINK) Education Working Group. Committee members are primarily federal librarians and others who hold positions in federal libraries and information centers. The third edition of the handbook has newly revised and updated chapters, sections, and information.

In keeping with the charge of the original task force, this handbook is a resource tool for librarians new to the federal community and a quick reference guide for established federal librarians. Because the *Handbook of Federal Librarianship* is a guide written for professional librarians, it not intended to be a manual on how to be a librarian. Instead, it focuses on the federal angle of otherwise standard practices and procedures of good librarianship. This edition omitted topics if it did not contain any uniquely federal characteristics. The copyright chapter is an exception to this rule because it remains a challenging and continuously developing topic for all librarians. The Education Working Group overwhelmingly favored producing this handbook in electronic format so that working group members can update it as often as new developments or issues emerge.

To avoid duplicating information already available elsewhere, the working group identified a large body of existing resources and an extensive existing collection on this topic. Therefore, this handbook provides only brief treatment of the main points of a topic with hypertext links to web sites for detailed coverage and references to print publications. The final selection of the handbook has a comprehensive listing with hypertext links and bibliographic citations in the Resources chapter. To suggest additions or changes to this handbook, please send an email to fliccfpe@loc.gov.

Acknowledgements

The FEDLINK Education Working Group would like to acknowledge the 40 librarians who volunteered to work on this third version. While not everyone was able to devote the time required to be a member of the Handbook committee, many of the suggestions, recommendations, and referrals were essential to the completion of the handbook. The working group is also grateful to previous taskforce members who conceived of this book and provided a strong foundation for this edition. Although the handbook does not list many of their names, it still uses some of their original wording and organization.

Special thanks go to

Dianne Schnurrpusch who lead the project revise and update the handbook.
Carol Ramkey for spearheading the new and improved Introduction Chapter;
Jennifer McMahan for giving new life to the Reference and Referral Chapter;
Teri Devoe for taking the lead on the Collections and Resources Chapter;
Nancy Faget for coordinating revision of the Federal Depository Library Chapter with GPO;
Trudie Root for writing the new Library Management Chapter;
FEDLINK staff for revising the FEDLINK Chapter;
Vakare Valaitis for updating the Copyright Management Chapter;
Kim Edwin for countless hours selecting information sources and services for the Resources Chapter, and all of the colleagues, staff, friends, and everyone who participated in virtual meetings and online collaborations or reviewed, edited, keyed, and/or proofread parts of the handbook.

Federal Library and Information Center Committee Education Working Group

Meg Tulloch, National Defense University, Chair

Committee Members and Contributors

Christine Baker
Food and Drug Administration
Silver Spring, MD

Sally Bosken
U.S. Naval Observatory
Washington, DC

Clark Brown
Federal Library and Information Network (FEDLINK)
Washington, DC

Lizzie Daniels
Federal Library and Information Network (FEDLINK)
Washington, DC

Blane K. Dessy
Federal Library and Information Network (FEDLINK)
Washington, DC

Teri Devoe
Institute of Museum and Library Services
Washington, DC

Kim Edwin
Library of Congress
Washington, DC

Nancy Faget
Army Research Laboratory
Adelphi, MD

George Franchois
Department of the Interior
Washington, DC

Roger Garren
Department of State
Washington, DC

Kathleen Hanselmann
Defense Language Institute
Monterey, CA

Robin Harvey
Federal Library and Information Network (FEDLINK)
Washington, DC

Georgette Harris
Federal Library and Information Network (FEDLINK)
Washington, DC

Elinda Harris Deans
Federal Library and Information Network (FEDLINK)
Washington, DC

Anne Harrison
Federal Library and Information Network (FEDLINK)
Washington, DC

Marlena Jones
Federal Library and Information Network (FEDLINK)
Washington, DC

Lori Kearse
Federal Library and Information Network (FEDLINK)
Washington, DC

Holly Kerwin
Federal Library and Information Network (FEDLINK)
Washington, DC

Sherry Kish
Department of State
Washington, DC

Carol Lucke
Naval Research Laboratory
Washington, DC

Lynn McDonald
Federal Library and Information Network (FEDLINK)
Washington, DC

Michael McDonald
Internal Revenue Service
Washington, DC

Barbara McDougald
U. S. Patent and Trademark Office
Alexandria, VA

Connie McEowen
Army Research Laboratory
Adelphi, MD

Jennifer McMahan
Department of Justice
Washington, DC

Colleen Pritchard
Food and Drug Administration
Silver Spring, MD

Carol Ramkey
U.S. Marine Corps University
Quantico, VA

Donna Ramsey
Van Noy Library
Fort Belvoir, VA

Trudie Root
Army Library Program (ALP)
Washington, DC

Diane Schnurrpusch
Defense Technical Information Center
Fort Belvoir, VA

Helen Sherman
Defense Technical Information Center
Fort Belvoir, VA

Meg Tulloch
National Defense University
Washington, DC

Vakare Valaitis
Defense Technical Information Center
Fort Belvoir, VA

Table of Contents

I. Introduction

By Carol Ramkey, Nancy Faget, Sara Walch, Michelle Lubatti, and Diane Schnurrpusch

To further an understanding of the duties and procedures of a federal librarian, the first step is to describe federal libraries and information centers and explain how they support their parent organizations, cover civil service procedures, and offer tips for learning about the unique aspects of federal employment.

Federal Libraries

Federal libraries and information centers are as diverse as those in the non-federal realm are. They range from well-known, national libraries and repositories to one-person units for a specific subject. They include organizations specializing in science, technology, medicine, transportation, law, intelligence, culture, and in the environment, monetary and financial systems, national defense, education, and much more.

The variety in federal libraries also includes the populations served. Most support federal agencies and their employees while some libraries assist academic communities or provide for military members and their families. Many also serve the public. Federal libraries also vary in the ways they perform their missions. Some hold vast collections of physical objects and interact with many of their users in person. On the opposite end are digital libraries, which communicate exclusively with their customers by phone or electronically. The majority of federal libraries and information centers fall somewhere in the middle.

Despite their multiplicity, federal libraries hold several commonalities. They each support one branch of the federal government – legislative, judicial, or executive, and receive federal funds.

Federal Librarians – Life with the Civil Service

Office of Personnel Management (OPM)

OPM is responsible for managing many, but not all aspects of the federal personnel or Civil Service process. One of its primary goals is to ensure that federal employees are hired and promoted based on merit and qualifications rather than as part of political spoils. As part of this process, OPM established and maintains job descriptions and qualifications for civilian white collar jobs on the General Schedule and trade, craft and labor jobs, on the Wage Grade, [not covered here]. Supervisory positions, in which 25 percent or more of the duties involves supervision of federal workers, are graded by the General Schedule Supervisory Guide.)

OPM also establishes regulations overseeing the recruitment, hiring and management of federal employees, classifies and groups similar jobs into numerical occupational series and pay grades and also issues qualification guidelines for federal jobs in specific series. The federal pay schedules are largely set by the series classification guidelines and positions, and even people, are frequently referred to by their occupational series numbers (e.g. "I'm a 1410, what are you? I'm a 341.") and/or their grade level (e.g. "She's a 14." or "He's a 9.")

Classification pertains to a position or job and the evaluation process that determines the appropriate pay system, occupational series, title, and grade/pay band.

Qualifications pertain to a person and describe the knowledge skills and/or abilities a person must have to be successful in a particular occupation.

Position Classification Standards follow a set format and a formula of graduated points based on the degree of difficulty, complexity, and autonomy based on nine factors:

1. Knowledge required by the position
2. Supervisory controls
3. Guidelines
4. Complexity
5. Scope and effect
6. Personal contacts
7. Purpose of contacts
8. Physical demands
9. Work environment

Knowing and understanding the formulas used in the classification standards helps explain why certain positions have certain grades. (Note: Qualification standards describe the minimum qualification requirements (for example, educational, medical, age, experience, etc.) for each occupational series. These are the standards used by OPM and other agency hiring officials to determine which applicants are eligible for a specific position and salary.

The 1400 Series consists of:
    Librarians -1410: Classification and Qualification Standards
    Archivists - 1420: Classification and Qualification Standards
    Technical Information Specialists (TIS) -1412: Classification and Qualification Standards
    Library Technicians – 1411: Classification Standards *
    Archival Technicians – 1421: Classification Standards *
    *Library and Archival Technicians do not have unique qualification standards; their qualification standards fall under the Group Coverage Qualification Standards for Clerical and Administrative Support Positions.

The classification standards for the 1400 series are quite outdated; the 1410, 1411 and 1412 were last updated in 1994, the 1420 in 2005, and the 1421 in 1968! Unfortunately, this means the descriptions and rankings of duties and factors are very outdated.

The 1400 series is a small one; there are probably fewer than 5,000 people occupying this series within the federal government as compared to General Administrative, Clerical and Office Services (300 series), which has tens of thousands of positions. Because of the small size of this occupational series the chances of OPM updating the 1400 series classification and qualification standards are slim.

Because there are so few federal jobs in the 1400 series, librarians, archivists, technical information specialists and library/archival technicians who restrict their job hunt to the 1400 series may find it hard to find positions or to move and be promoted within the federal government. By broadening their search to other job series, they may find more job opportunities in areas like

    Knowledge Manager (usually in the 301, 341, 343 series)
    Website Manager (2210 series)
    Intelligence Analyst (301, 341, 198 series)
    Social Media Manager
    Records Manager (301, 341 series)
    Public Affairs
    Information Technology

Program Analyst or Manager (340 series)
Freedom of Information Act (FOIA) Manager

When applying for positions outside the 1400 series, applicants need to translate knowledge, skills, abilities, and work experience into the language of the job description. Instead of using technical library or archive jargon, applications should refer to the terms used in the description of duties and qualifications for the job and use those words to describe experience and accomplishments.

Competencies and professional development

Competencies are patterns of skills, knowledge, abilities, behaviors, and other characteristics (intrinsic or acquired) that an individual needs to perform work roles or occupational functions successfully. These patterns create a common bond of understanding and a common language for defining professional standards. Competencies are also the foundation for competency-based management and continuous process improvement, ensuring that federal librarians have the knowledge, skills, and abilities to accomplish mission requirements. They may be organized in a framework that differentiates increasing stages of expertise. Competencies are the combination of

- ψ Knowledge – knowing about or understanding something, something learned by either study or experience;
- ψ Skill – the ability to perform or accomplish something; knowing how to do something;
- ψ Ability – the capacity to do something; an inherent mental or physical characteristic that helps someone do certain things.

Competencies are different from performance standards, which establish qualitative or quantitative measures for evaluating work performance, or and duty statements, which describe tasks or processes undertaken to accomplish one's work.

Individuals can use competencies to
- ψ determine continuing education needs,
- ψ set goals for advancement,
- ψ discuss performance, career aspirations, and development needs with management, or
- ψ create a professional development plan.

Organizations can use competencies for
- ψ strategic planning and budget execution,
- ψ recruiting and hiring,
- ψ performance feedback and management,
- ψ training and development,
- ψ career development,
- ψ succession management, or
- ψ alignment with the agency's mission and strategic goals.

Although OPM has moved away from using the common phrase "Knowledge, Skills and Abilities" or "KSAs" in job announcements or requiring applicants to write essays about their KSAs, it still supports the concept of a competency-based workforce.

The **Fedlink Human Resources Working Group** developed and published the *FLICC Competencies for Federal Librarians*. It bases its competencies on the larger librarian and information science profession and focuses on the particular competencies needed by federal librarians and information professionals. Librarians and information professionals can use it as a working document throughout their careers.

In addition to using the competencies for professional development, many federal librarians have found membership in professional organizations has helped their development and promotion potential. For a list of professional organizations in which federal librarians are frequent members, see the Resources Chapter at the end of this book.

FEDLINK also provides training and educational opportunities for federal librarians and information professionals.

Getting Started

Once an applicant has identified or has been offered a position in the federal library and information center arena, preparing for the interview or on the first day of the job is a high priority. Prospective and newly hired can also find avenues for joining the community of federal librarians. There are many free magazines and Web sites specific to federal employees and field discussion lists, professional development opportunities, and communication options as well.

Rules and Regulations

Federal employees should become familiar with the regulations of the branch of government in which they work, executive, legislative, and judicial, as well as the regulations of specific agencies and libraries. Federal regulations pertaining to federal employees can be found in Title 5 U.S. Code - Government Organization and Employees and in Title 5 Code of Federal Regulations (CFR) - Administrative Personnel. In addition, most agencies promulgate rules and regulations for employees with an agency-specific title of the CFR. In addition to these, many federal libraries have individual policies and procedures governing library's operations. Some libraries have authorization to establish the library through legislation, internal policy, regulation, or memorandum. The Department of the Interior is one example; it was established by Secretarial Order No.1173 dated April 28, 1937 and No.2525, Section 1, dated June 24, 1949.

The history and mission statement of the library, the agency organizational chart, and the annual report are also sources for the library's position in the context of the agency, is budgeting and funding information. While the organizational chart shows structure (Reference, Circulation, Cataloging, Acquisitions, etc.) and staff positions (federal and/or contract personnel), information on library services (e.g., bibliographies, factsheets, path finders, end user training, etc.), patrons (e.g., agency personnel, the public, etc.) and resources (e.g., print, electronic, special collections) are also helpful for new employees.

If your position is not exempt from collective bargaining, new employees need to understand their rights and responsibilities as a union member. The three major labor unions for federal employees are the American Federation of Government Employees (AFGE), the National Federation of Federal Employees (NFFE), and the National Association of Government Employees (NAGE).

OPM also offers detailed information on federal personnel matters (salaries and wages, leave policies, benefits, travel, etc.) are found its Web site.

Background Checks and Security Clearances

All federal positions require background checks. Although a basic background is "voluntary," all applicants must agree to the check if he/she seeks a federal position. OPM performs background checks and offer a fact sheet for additional information. Most background checks occur after a person has a tentatively offered position and before employment begins.

Certain jobs, especially within the defense, intelligence, nuclear and financial regulatory and oversight agencies, require additional security clearances for both federal employees and contractors. The requirement and level of clearance is related to the position and cannot be negotiated by a job applicant. In some cases, individuals report for work while the additional clearance paperwork is processed. If the clearance is not authorized, the person will be removed from the job.

The names, paperwork, and processes for these clearances vary depending on the agency and the level of the clearance. OPM initiates the process and explains the process to the applicant or holder of any position requiring a clearance. Once a clearance is granted, it stays active whether the person stays in the original position or not. Periodically clearances become inactive (usually every 3 -10 years) and have to be renewed. Because people with active clearances have an edge in the job application process, federal job applicants often ask if they can get a clearance to improve their hiring chances. Only OPM or a hiring agency, however, can initiate a clearance.

II. Reference and Referral

By Jennifer McMahan and Diane Schnurrpusch

This chapter discusses tips and best practices for providing reference and referral, as well as interlibrary loan (ILL) services in federal libraries. Whether your library serves the public or focuses on internal user group, you are likely to field a wide array of requests common to all institutions. Organizations may receive general information, ready reference, referral, and research requests.

Reference and Referral Requests

For general information requests, librarians may create frequently asked questions lists (FAQs) to answer "how to" questions that are related to a specific library or collection. Consider posting FAQs on your agency's website or intranet so users can find answers immediately. Answers to ready reference questions often require consulting one or two print or online reference resources. With the focus and mission of the organization in mind, develop bibliographies or Web-based subject guides to help users through research topics and give them efficient access to ready reference sources. Larger research requests require a reference interview to clarify the scope of what information the user needs. For complex requests, multiple interactions may be required to ascertain the information needs of the user. Responses to research projects could be in the form of a report of findings, or a custom bibliography for further research.

At times, a question may be too technical or outside of the organization's scope. Other times, the person making the request is outside the authorized user community. In these instances, an internal list or database of subject matter experts (SME), libraries, or online resources will save the requester and the library time and offer the requester options for locating the needed information.

Often, when there are no materials in the collection on a specific topic, other federal libraries and information centers may have the resources required in their collections. The scope of subjects covered by federal collections is both vast and developing. For a selection of the print and electronic publications available in the federal community, refer to the library collections listed in the Resources chapter of the handbook.

For those new to reference services, the Reference and User Services Association (RUSA) of the American Library Association (ALA) offers general tips to responding to inquiries in their "Guidelines for Behavioral Performance of Reference and Information Service Providers".

Barriers and Information Access

There are various reasons why librarians in the federal system may have trouble accessing the information needed to serve their customers. Federal libraries that are completely or partially contracted out might be limited in resources they can access. Another barrier could be lack of funding, as commercial databases with unique and valuable content can be quite expensive. Federal library employees might also find their access to resources blocked due to security protocols on their networks.

One way to overcome these barriers is to reach out to other federal libraries and nonprofit organizations. FEDLINK's Federal Library Directory provides over 1,000 library contacts. Many agency libraries have public Web sites including information on collections, contact information, online catalog, or even an "Ask a Librarian" service. Local electronic mail lists and networks are another avenue for getting assistance from colleagues. While public libraries can be good resources, most subscription database usage agreements do not allow using public library databases to work on behalf of a company or government agency.

Limited Access Resources

Federal librarians can use limited access resources by providing proof of federal employment, typically with a .gov or .mil email address. In addition to internal content, some sites also provide access to commercial databases. State and local government databases are another resource for materials. For example, federal employees can open accounts to access Texas Secretary of State corporation records for free. Other suggested resources are

- ψ R&E Gateway
- ψ Defense Manpower Data Center (DMDC) Data Request System
- ψ ASSIST – Military Specifications and Standards
- ψ NASA Aeronautics & Space Database (NA&SD) - Registration Required
- ψ NATO Standardization Agency (URL to request access to protected site)
- ψ Homeland Security Digital Library
- ψ Intelink
- ψ OpenSource.gov (English translations of foreign media)

Privacy and Security Concerns

Protect the privacy of the requester. When considering reaching outside the agency for assistance with information requests, always ask the requester first. Only collect Personally Identifiable Information (PII) according to protocols set by the agency and be familiar with the Privacy Act, which regulates the public's right to know what information an agency has collected and allows individuals to request that information.

Protect information. Whether an agency-only library or a federal library open to the public, be sure not to provide any classified or sensitive information, Seek permission from a supervisor or agency public affairs officer before complying with an outside request. Keep information on FOIA contacts for the agency handy to refer requesters to the appropriate offices. Take care when transmitting information that is not publicly available.

Some agencies also prohibited employees from identifying an affiliation with a particular agency on public sites such as Facebook or LinkedIn. The use of .gov or .mil email addresses may also be restricted.

Serving the Public

Some federal libraries are open to the public, either without restriction, or by appointment only. Some might provide a public reading room (for example, the Nuclear Regulatory Commission and the Library of Congress), as well as on-site or virtual research assistance.

Balance services to internal employees with serving the public. Federal libraries may have to refer routine questions to public or academic libraries, or to more appropriate agencies. Reserve your resources for questions about unique resources that only your organization can answer.

Laws have been enacted which improve citizen access to government information and services. Read about the FOIA and E-gov Acts.

Visitor assistance – You may have to assist with photo id, registration, physical scanning, etc. To protect your collection, your library may have restrictions on what the patron can bring into or take out of the library, especially in archives or rare book rooms.

Virtual Reference

The fact that many libraries have branches all over the world, plus customers all over the world means that reference librarians in the government may have to work differently to cover the hours. Additionally, due to the nature of some agency work, such as defense, homeland security, and law enforcement, some librarians may work weekends and nights at times to support the mission. For example, Senate librarians are available when Congress is in session, no matter how late; some Department of Defense librarians act as "back-up" support during military exercises. Since the federal government encourages telework, both the librarian and the user may also be working from somewhere other than their primary location.

For these reasons and others, most federal libraries provide some kind of "virtual reference" service to their patrons.

What is virtual reference?

According to the Reference & User Services Association (RUSA), "Virtual reference is reference service initiated electronically, often in real-time, where patrons employ computers or other Internet technology to communicate with reference staff, without being physically present." Communication methods used in virtual reference include chat, videoconferencing, Voice over IP, co-browsing, e-mail, texting, and instant messaging. While libraries often use online sources to provide virtual reference, use of electronic sources in seeking answers is not of itself virtual reference. RUSA also provides guidelines for implementing and maintaining virtual reference services.

Virtual reference systems and features

One type of virtual reference system is a Customer Relations Management (CRM) software application. There are several on the market and although we won't discuss brand names here, a CRM can be thought of as a software application through which a library's reference staff receives, tracks, and answers reference questions coming into the library through email, phone, web form, and walk in customers. The staff can also use these products to compile Frequently Asked Questions (FAQs) into a knowledge base for future use; delete personally identifiable information (PII) to protect the privacy of the customer; and produce statistical reports on the number and topic of questions answered for a given period. All of these tools can be very useful in helping a library streamline its operations and quantify its value to a parent agency.

The Department of Justice Library uses a software system hosted by a vendor to provide basic email reference through an "Ask a Librarian" service. At the U.S. Patent and Trademark Office, the library has developed a very sophisticated CRM online system for communicating with thousands of patent examiners so they can share documents, links, and other resources. These systems offer far more capability than general email systems and keep a record of each interaction.

Some agencies use knowledge bases to keep track of FAQs or infrequent queries so that information can be easily retrieved. The Defense Technical Information Center (DTIC) reference team stores its Standard Operating Procedures (SOPs) and numerous facts, contact information, links, and more on an internal wiki. The Supreme Court Library has a database of all requests (regardless of format) going back for years. Some federal libraries are using Sharepoint™ to catalog requests and generate statistical reports.

Any collaborative tool can work well, particularly if it is searchable.

Interlibrary Loan

Most federal libraries do not loan directly to the public, but do loan to other libraries. Other federal libraries borrow, but do not loan to anyone. Many libraries will lend for free to government libraries, and government libraries generally do not charge to lend themselves. Academic libraries are the exception, as they often charge unless there is an agreement in place.

There are a number of options for making interlibrary loan requests:

- ψ OCLC
- ψ Other specialized networks, for example, DOCLINE – for libraries with medical/scientific journal collections.
- ψ ALA Form. Fact Sheet

As with reference requests, make sure that any items lent are not sensitive or classified in nature.

III. Resources/Collections

By Teri Devoe, Sally Boskin, Kathleen Hanselmann, and Colleen Pritchard

How to Build User-Centered Collections

Identifying the Users

The first step in building user-centered collections is to identify the library's various user groups. One basic starting point for identifying potential users is a review of the organization's website and/or intranet site. In addition to offering an overview of existing programmatic areas, websites often point to the organization's mission, strategic plan, and emerging initiatives. Depending on these characteristics, the library may have a case for reaching out to the general public as well as serving staff within the institution.

Over time, librarians may build liaison relationships with various offices throughout the institution that can help them identify and reach out to other user groups. Human resource departments are an excellent starting point as are senior-level managers responsible for multiple work teams. With experience, reference desk staff will also develop a broad understanding of institutional needs and should be an obvious resource for identifying user groups within the library itself.

Determining User Needs

There is no single path to understanding the needs of existing or potential library users. Qualitative methods such as informal conversations, feedback mechanisms and focus groups should be considered along with quantitative mechanisms, such as surveys, user studies and usage statistics. Library size and scale can play an enormous role in the nature of this information-gathering. Some libraries can successfully circulate publication catalogs among their user groups, and some information professionals are physically embedded in work teams, lending them an intimate knowledge of user needs. Other libraries serve thousands of remote patrons and are better equipped to disseminate online surveys or examine data logs to understand their various user segments. Keeping these limitations in mind, librarians should strive to collect user feedback in as many ways as possible and document it systematically. Inevitably, library budgets will limit the quantity of newly acquired materials and ongoing subscriptions. Being able to triangulate feedback from a number of different sources can lend some credibility to the task of prioritizing purchases.

User-expressed needs are an obvious resource for building and managing collections, but librarians may also look beyond their immediate institutions in the name of building stronger collections. Many librarians still consult discipline-specific bibliographies to fill collection gaps and/or compare local collections with those of peer institutions. Librarians may also base purchases on the reputation of publishers, journal impact factors, and the availability of consortia to help offset costs. Now more than ever, librarians must understand the cost-benefit relationship for emerging formats and new purchasing models, which may allow them to shift from a just-in-case collection development model to a just-in-time one. All of these factors should be considered when building a collection around user needs.

Establishing a Collection Development Policy

Once patron needs are assessed, the librarian's next step is to formalize an approach to collection management decisions. The main reason to write a collection development policy is to create a planning, allocation, informational, administrative and training document. It should describe the library's purpose for building a collection, selecting and deselecting materials and purchasing different materials. In the event of library staff turnover or reorganization, the collection development policy codifies collecting priorities and offers a roadmap for collection management decisions. Thus, it is an essential internal management tool for the library.

The collection development policy will also explain and defend the library's plan for providing necessary access to information resources for the community it serves. In this sense, it also addresses audiences that are external to the library, from senior managers to donors of materials.

To write a good policy, it is essential to understand the local information ecosystem and other sources of information, whether informal colleague networks that extend beyond borders and agencies, other libraries in the area or cooperation in library networks. These sources will naturally affect the library's collecting decisions. For example, if an expensive run of journals is available in the local university science library, it may be redundant to actively collect another set. These considerations need to be spelled out in the policy.

For an example of a federal library collection development policy and plan, see the Base Library RAF Lakenheath UK examples in the appendix.

Other examples of federal library collection development policies include:
- Φ Rochester Public Library Collection Development Policy
- Φ Australian Libraries Guidelines for the Preparation of a Collection Development Policy
- Φ British Library Collection Development Policy

Format Considerations

Utilizing the collection development policy as a guide, library staff should strive to provide an effective combination of print, non-print and electronic resources for their users. By making informed decisions on the format needs of the collection, they will better serve patrons and add value to the agency. As with other considerations, format decisions may be dependent on the availability of funds.

Many libraries offer collections in a variety of formats:
> ***Printed monographs, reports, serials.*** According to the Library of Congress, serials are print or non-print publications issued in parts, usually bearing issue numbers and/or dates. A serial is expected to continue indefinitely. Serials include magazines, newspapers, annuals (such as reports, yearbooks, and directories), journals, memoirs, proceedings, transactions of societies, and monographic series.

Monograph considerations:
- ψ Hardbound or softbound
- ψ Language
- ψ Availability of other formats for core titles, i.e., e-books
- ψ Any exceptions, i.e., study guides, textbooks

Serial Considerations:
- ψ Subscription only versus purchasing individual issues
- ψ Title represents a permanent addition to the collection
- ψ Indexed or abstracted
- ψ Demonstrated need as evidenced by document delivery statistics
- ψ Scholarly reputation of the journal
- ψ Price
- ψ Vendor

Electronic Resources. According to the AACR2, 2005 Update, electronic resources are materials encoded for manipulation by a computerized device, which may require the use of a peripheral (e.g., CD-ROM drive) or a connection to a computer network (e.g., the Internet). This definition does **not** include electronic resources that do not **require** the use of a computer, for example, music compact discs and videodiscs

Examples of electronic resources include:
- ψ Indexing and abstracting databases
- ψ Full-text aggregated databases
- ψ E-journals
- ψ E-books

Since these resources typically represent the most expensive category of materials, it is highly recommended that a resource evaluation trial be established prior to purchasing an electronic resource. Many libraries formulate a separate collection policy for electronic resources due to their inherent challenges including management, discovery, delivery, usage statistics, and maintenance. Libraries are challenged with balancing print and electronic acquisitions as part of the collection development workflow.

E-books are becoming very popular and bring with them a myriad of issues including:
- ψ Format appropriate for patrons' needs?
- ψ Access point - catalog in the OPAC?
- ψ Interface issues
- ψ Device incompatibilities
- ψ Mobile applications? E-reader software?
- ψ Lending issues
- ψ Privacy issues
- ψ Timing for the release of print and electronic format
- ψ E-books available in a particular discipline
- ψ Pricing for electronic titles is almost always more expensive
- ψ Purchase individual titles or a package
- ψ Copyright

An excellent resource that addresses the complexities of electronic resources is **The Kovacs Guide to Electronic Library Collection Development: Essential Core Subject Collections, Selection Criteria, and Guidelines**. 2nd ed. New York, NY: Neal Schulman Publishers, 2009. 300 pages.

Criteria to consider when acquiring electronic resources:
- ψ Trial available along with vendor training
- ψ Adherence to Agency IT guidelines and approval processes, including 508 compliance and special software/hardware needs
- ψ Web or CD-ROM access to resource
- ψ Firewall constraints
- ψ Site license model - available for remote access, sites configuration? Unlimited access or specified number of users or limited number of downloads
- ψ Vendor reliability and performance; customer service availability
- ψ Electronic access mimics the print counterpart (e.g., illustrations, charts)?
- ψ Perpetual access or limitations
- ψ Mode of authentication – IP or password, proxy server
- ψ Availability of usage stats with COUNTER
- ψ Mobile applications
- ψ Library customization and branding availability
- ψ Pricing for bundled formats (print and online)

Videorecordings and sound recordings
- ψ The Library of Congress notes the following:
  - Φ **Compact Disc Formats**: • Dual Discs • Mini CDs • Mini Discs • SACD • Shaped Discs
  - Φ **DVD Formats:** • CD/DVD Combos • Dual Discs • DVD Audio
  - Φ **Electronic Resources:** • CD-ROMs • Midi Files • MP3 Files
- ψ For a good overview of digital formats and evaluation factors see Formats, Evaluation Factors, and Relationships (Sustainability of Digital Formats - Planning for Library of Congress Collections)
- ψ Microform types include microfilm, microfiche, and microcards. These formats require the use of special reader machines and may have limited longevity. It is often the only format for dissertations or serial backfiles and is often acquired when the material is not available in another format. Options for converting microforms to digital format do exist. For more on microforms see the Library of Congress Microforms MARC 21 Format for Bibliographic Data

Over the years, publishing trends have shifted from print to electronic journals. The 24/7 online availability is very attractive to library customers who work remotely or do not have access to the physical library. Many libraries have shifted their print subscriptions to electronic formats, especially as some libraries have been forced to reduce their physical footprint. Some libraries have moved older collections to an offsite storage facility or have formed consortia for document delivery solutions. Other libraries have moved to purchasing electronic backfiles as they eliminate print serials.

However, not all resources are available in electronic formats and many agree that it is important to maintain original print copies in the case of digitized versions of materials. The National Library of Medicine has made plans to provide a framework for a national print retention program to ensure continued access to the historical literature. To learn more about this effort, see NLM and NN/LM National Cooperative Medical Journals Print Retention Program

Preservation

LC Preservation Resources
The appendix includes preservation resources from the Library of Congress including
- ψ Library of Congress FLICC / Preservation Directorate Readings
- ψ FLICC Insititute for Library Technicians II: Emergency Management Resource List
- ψ FLICC Preservation Webcasts/Podcasts

Other Preservation Societies, etc.
The appendix also includes preservation resources from other groups, including
- ψ Council on Library and Information Resources, National Institute of Standards and Technology, Guide for Librarians and Archivists: Care and Handling of CDs and DVDs

How to Obtain Materials

Acquisition Resources
The purpose of acquisitions in federal libraries is the same as in all libraries: to identify, select, acquire, and provide access to publications, electronic materials, and any other format or type of information materials needed to fulfill the mission of the library and its larger authoritative body. The acquisitions process combines locating appropriate library materials, finding the lowest possible prices, providing access to materials, and sharing resources among libraries. These functions must be carried out by following standard U.S. government agency procurement practices and policies that local agency procurement authorities require. They are almost always carried out through the use of the appropriate statutory authority (such as Federal Acquisition Regulation (FAR), the U.S. Code Economy Act (31 U.S.C. §§ 1535 and 1536) and the Federal Acquisitions Streamlining Act (FASA).

Acquisitions Policies
Library acquisitions personnel must also maintain high standards in their purchasing, automate and integrate their acquisition efforts, establish and maintain cooperative and resource sharing activities, and stay abreast of new trends and issues in library science. For an overview of an acquisitions course see the American Library Association (ALA). The Association for Library Collections & Technical Services Acquisitions Section of ALA has adopted a Statement on Principles and Standards of Acquisitions Practice. It outlines the basic doctrines that should guide the actions and policies of library acquisitions units and individual personnel.

Library of Congress Acquisition Resources
The Library of Congress is tasked with one of the most extensive acquisition and collection development missions among federal libraries. They use six methods to acquire materials: Cataloging in Publication, Copyright, Exchange, Gift, Federal Transfer, and Purchase. The collection is shaped by the Library's acquisitions department. The following links include information about Library of Congress acquisitions policies:

International exchange service
Donation/Exchange of Books & Other Library Materials
Overseas Operations & Cooperative Acquisitions

Document Delivery

Document delivery suppliers acquire copies of published or unpublished materials in print or electronic format in response to a library's request for a specific item. Vendors can provide individual magazine or journal articles, reports, documents, dissertations, theses, and other types of materials. They accept orders electronically, by fax, and by phone. Many firms specialize in same-day rush delivery. The service is priced on a per-document basis. Usually, there is a flat basic fee to retrieve and deliver the document; this fee may be higher for rush or special delivery. In addition to the basic fee, the vendor may pass through any copyright royalty charges assessed by the copyright owner, and may charge an additional per-page or per-document fee for photocopying, faxing, or other special services. Document delivery vendors may offer volume discounts for multiple copy orders or for organizations that routinely order many documents during the year.

Document suppliers frequently operate on a deposit account system, where funds are transferred in advance to the supplier and orders are deducted from the amount on deposit until funds are exhausted. FEDLINK offers document delivery services. See the FEDLINK section for further information and for the names and descriptions of specific vendors.

Example of a federal library's written document delivery policy:

- ψ When materials are not available through free interlibrary loan channels, they can be borrowed or copied through fee-based services as permitted by local policies and budgets.
- ψ Document delivery services may be especially useful when requests for copies of articles exceed the quantities defined under the CONTU guidelines for interlibrary loan. These delivery services collect the copyright fee as well as a photocopy fee, although other means of copyright protection may be utilized.
- ψ Payment Options for Document Delivery Services
    - Φ The library can set up a FEDLINK account for both interlibrary loan fee payments and document delivery.
    - Φ Deposit accounts can be used as allowed. Such accounts are generally available through agencies such as the National Technical Information Service (NTIS) and the Government Printing Office (GPO), as well as some commercial services.

Agency-specific considerations

Most libraries seek to provide all of their users with the information they need, when they need it. However, the reality of budget-related issues and materials availability prevents most libraries from reaching the ideal of this goal.

Each agency approaches acquisitions from a slightly different perspective. In many libraries, selecting and acquiring materials may be combined in the same department—in the smallest libraries perhaps even by the same person. In larger libraries, a collection development department or designated subject specialists may take responsibility for selection. In essence, acquisitions is the business side of bringing materials into the library or licensing access to library resources.

Some agencies use book wholesalers (or jobbers) who provide a central channel for acquiring trade and professional books in all subject areas: textbooks, government documents, association publications, foreign books, and other specialized publications. Although this category is called "books," the vendors provide materials in many different formats—hardcover and softcover books, technical reports, reprints, out-of-print titles, videos, sound recordings, and other audio-visuals, books on CD-ROM, large print or Braille materials, etc. Usually, book jobbers offer significant discounts from publishers' list price. They are able to supply popular titles, locate specialized or difficult-to-find materials and provide advance information about forthcoming titles. FEDLINK offers access to book wholesalers. See the FEDLINK section for further information and for the names of vendors with their specialties.

Libraries may establish a collaborative exchange with other organizations to provide in house documents in exchange for organizational documents relevant to the agency's mission. This is an excellent cost saving situation. There is also the potential for coordinating the acquisition of materials via collaborative purchases and resource sharing with other Federal agencies. For example, the Navy libraries collectively purchase online access to databases shared by all.

Other libraries use a government credit card to purchase books online through vendors or directly from publisher's websites. If a book is needed instantly, libraries can download a copy from a website and pay with credit card or walk to the book store. Offering instant access to both hardcover and e-books makes for happy patrons.

Example of a federal library's written acquisitions policy:

- ψ Libraries will acquire materials quickly, efficiently, and at the least expense, within the bounds of their respective Statements of Work and budgetary limitations.
- ψ Libraries will follow all applicable procurement regulations for purchasing materials.
- ψ Libraries generally purchase trade and commercial publications from a vendor, but may also make direct purchases from a publisher.
- ψ Libraries generally order journals and serials through a subscription agent, but may also make direct purchases from a publisher.
- ψ Libraries may establish accounts with book and journal vendors through FEDLINK.
- ψ Libraries may set up deposit accounts with other government agencies.
- ψ Government documents, including individual titles and periodicals, may be ordered through a deposit account with the Government Printing Office (GPO) or from the National Technical Information Service (NTIS).

Donations to the library

Donated books can help the library grow its collection. Unfortunately, most libraries cannot accept all of the books that they receive by donation. All libraries should have a written policy for donations that states specifically what the library will accept, i.e.: "The Library accepts donations of books, DVDs, and CDs; we do not accept school textbooks or materials in poor condition. The Library cannot arrange for book pickups." Make sure the patron also understands that the library does not automatically add donated books to its collection. The donation policy should include information about what happens when a book is not added to the collection. It may be helpful to maintain a list of other places donors could consider. Libraries should also plan proactively for what to do with donations that are not added to the collection. They should decide whether or not donations are acknowledged and how (e.g., commemorative bookplate, note field in the card catalog: "gift of Joe Smith"). In some cases, the library may provide a letter of receipt that the donor fills out for tax purposes, but typically it will be up to the donor to assign a value for tax purposes. Many writers like to donate books they have authored, but libraries should use restraint when accepting them; the author will be able to say "my book is held in the ---library." Don't let library acceptance be an endorsement!

In general, the rules for accepting donations vary from agency to agency and organizations within the agencies. It may be that each librarian has to research this issue locally. For example, for donation to Navy libraries, the determination has to do with the value of the donation. If under a certain threshold, the library can accept it. If over, then the legal office would be involved. Be sure to know the rules and abide by them.

Example of a federal library's written policy on donations:
- ψ Libraries will establish local practices and procedures for accepting and processing donations of books, documents, or other library materials.
- ψ Libraries may receive donations from a variety of sources: staff, other libraries, other offices, other federal agencies.
- ψ In addition to general selection criteria above, libraries should also consider the following when selecting donations to be added to the collection:
    - Φ Information provided by the donor as to the significance of the work.
    - Φ Currency and condition of the material.
- ψ Libraries will reserve the right to refuse to add a donation or gift to the collection and to dispose

of any such item following established dispersal procedures if the donor does not want the item(s) returned.

ψ Libraries will not accept photocopies of books due to copyright concerns.

How to Dispose of Materials

Weeding/Deselection

Deselection is an important part of maintaining healthy library collections. An ongoing collection review for the systematic withdrawl of resources, based on the collection development policy, leads to a vital collection with increased usage. A weeding policy will be based on the mission and goals of the Agency, space concerns and other factors. It should include the cancellation of journal titles that are no longer in scope, the transfer of materials to storage, and exceptions to the policy such as titles that relate to the agency's history, those that have ongoing research value, or those used for training purposes.

Benefits of weeding include:

ψ Increased space to facilitate future growth
ψ Collection currency
ψ Ease of access for customers to find needed material
ψ Ability to identify missing, outdated, and worn materials that require replacement

Before embarking on a weeding project, libraries should check their holdings against any union catalogs or consortia. This will ensure that a weeded title is available via interlibrary loan if needed. Further, libraries should consult with subject specialists on the "classics" along with standard bibliographic aids.

There are different methods for weeding and classes available (e.g., Lyrasis). One benchmark tool is the Continuous Review Evaluation Weeding (CREW) Method, a landmark manual updated in 2008. The CREW Method uses a formula based on the 4C's – condition, copyright, content, and circulation.

Librarians can also consult ALA Library Factsheet 15 – Weeding Library Collections: A Selected Annotated Bibliography for Library Collection Development.

General Criteria for Weeding:

ψ Agency goals that drive the needs of customers
ψ Actual usage as evidenced by circulation and interlibrary loan guidelines, in-house usage, and guidance from subject specialists
ψ Funds available to purchase updated materials or replacement copies
ψ Type of library – archival, primary, research
ψ Projected use of materials
ψ More current information available on the Web; periodicals available in full-text
ψ Title available to borrow via interlibrary loan
ψ Material duplicative or redundant
ψ Outdated material
ψ Material worn out or shabby in appearance
ψ Format no longer supported
ψ Book part of a series; keep heavily used volume and withdraw the rest
ψ Space constraints
ψ Materials support training needs

Transfer

Once library material weeding is complete, there are several options for handling them in federal libraries, including transfer.

Example of a Federal library's written transfer policy:
- ψ Disposal of Library Materials. Follow these guidelines:
    - Φ Librarians coordinate with the Services Logistics staff for turn-in of obsolete or irreparably worn library materials to the Defense Reutilization Marketing Office (DRMO). Librarians must contact DRMO for current turn-in procedures or go to Disposition Services at the Defense Logistics Agency available at http://www.dispositionservices.dla.mil/ .
    - Φ Library directors coordinate with the command librarian to redistribute excess materials as well as library-specific supply items that are in usable condition. Send excess materials to Air Force, DoD, and other Federal libraries upon agreement by the accepting agency. Military library listservs may be used to offer excess materials.
    - Φ Libraries may not sell any materials purchased with appropriated funds (APF) or marked as Air Force property IAW DoD 4160.21-M, Defense Materiel Disposition Manual; AFI 34-204, Property Management; and AFMAN 23-110, Volume 2, Part 13. Libraries may only sell donated materials at Services sales.

Donations

Donation is another option for materials weeded from federal libraries. Under the provisions of 41 CFR 102-37 Subpart H, a library may donate to public bodies in lieu of abandonment/destruction, property that has no commercial value for which the estimated cost of continued care and handling would exceed the estimated proceeds from their sale.

The United States Book Exchange (USBE), a non-profit organization, accepts unwanted publications and makes them immediately available to member libraries to fill in gaps.

The USBE accepts scholarly publications in all fields published from 2008 to the present. To donate, a library can send all of their materials and pay the shipping fees or send USBE a list of titles. In turn, USBE will make the selection and pay the associated shipping fees.
A library can join USBE by selecting one of three membership levels and order publications online. Materials not selected by members transfer to the Donational Program where libraries in developing countries or libraries working under severe budget constraints may select titles at no charge except for postage.

The National Library of Medicine also coordinates a Journal Donation Program to ensure that multiple copies of important biomedical print materials are preserved in print form. DOCLINE libraries can use their web-based system to view needed titles. Those who donate receive an email confirmation as well as instructions for the National Library of Medicine-paid shipping fees.

In addition, library associations and organizations facilitate and provide information on donation programs including:

- ψ FEDLIB: Federal Librarians Discussion List
  Members post their excess or weeded material lists to the listserv and provide contact and shipping information.
- ψ American Library Association (ALA) Library Fact Sheet 12 ALA provides information on groups and organizations that process book donations.

Often times, a library will check with their local public library to see if they accept donations or offer weeded materials to their patrons. Be mindful of removing any library security tags before offering the books to internal patrons.

IV. Federal Depository Library Program

An important Government program helps safeguard one of our nation's strongest traditions: the public's right to know. Since Congress established the Federal Depository Library Program (FDLP) in 1813, the FDLP has collected, organized, and preserved information produced by the Federal Government and assisted people in locating and using it.

Libraries designated as Federal depositories provide local, no-fee access to information from all three branches of the Federal Government. Expert assistance in locating specific information is available at all locations from Government information librarians. Federal depository collections are available for use by everyone. Collections are available in print, microfiche, and electronic formats on a wide range of topics relevant to the public and to professionals, researchers, and students in almost every field.

Administered by the U.S. Government Printing Office (GPO), FDLP libraries are located within libraries of all types and sizes including academic, public, academic, law, and community college libraries, as well as Federal and state libraries. They are located in nearly every congressional district throughout the United States and its territories. Libraries in the FDLP are required to respond to the Biennial Survey of Depository Libraries every other year to report on conditions in the depository libraries, as required by law (44 USC §1909). The FDLP Desktop and the FDLP Community site contain news, information, and communication intended specifically for the depository libraries.

Brief History

The FDLP originated in the early 1800s by a joint resolution of Congress. The Printing Act of 1895 was a comprehensive and substantive revision of public printing laws, which established the parameters for the current FDLP and GPO's role in providing distribution and cataloging services for U.S. Government information.

FDLP Today

The depository program has grown into a geographically dispersed network of nearly 1,200 libraries. Members of Congress by law have designated these libraries as official depositories. With a few exceptions, all Congressional districts and territories of the United States have at least one Federal depository library.

There are 47 regional depository libraries which have agreed to receive all tangible publications available through the FDLP and retain them for permanent public access. The majority of the Federal depository libraries are selective, tailoring their selections of Government information products to meet their community's needs. These libraries have limited retention responsibilities.

Services from the FDLP

One of GPO's missions is to provide, in partnership with the Federal depository libraries, for perpetual, free, and ready public access to the print and digital publications of the Federal Government. GPO's Federal Digital System (FDsys) is an advanced search engine, preservation repository, and content management system for information from all three branches of the Federal Government. FDsys preserves, authenticates, manages, and delivers Federal content upon request.

FDsys provides free online access to official publications from all three branches of the Federal Government. Through FDsys, you are able to:

ψ **Search for documents and publications** FDsys provides advanced search capabilities and the ability to refine and narrow your search for quick access to the information you need.

ψ **Browse for documents and publications** FDsys offers browsing by collection, Congressional committee, date, and Government author.

ψ **Access metadata about documents and publications** FDsys provides information about Government publications in standard XML formats.

ψ **Download documents and publications in multiple renditions or file formats** With FDsys, users can download a single file or download content and metadata packaged together in a compressed file.

FDsys provides users with authenticated documents, which have an eagle image or "GPO Seal of Authenticity" on them. The seal assures users that the document is unaltered since GPO made it available through FDsys. FDsys offers access to about 50 different collections of Government information. Some popular FDsys collections include:

Congressional Materials such as
    ψ Congressional Hearings
    ψ Bills & Laws
    ψ House & Senate Manuals
    ψ Presidential Publications such as
    ψ Public Papers of the Presidents
    ψ Budget of U.S. Government
    ψ Economic Report of the President
    ψ Federal Agency Resources such as
    ψ Federal Register
    ψ U.S. Government Manual

The Catalog of United States Government Publications (CGP) is GPO's Web-based bibliographic (catalog records) database of all formats of Federal publications. The database dates back to the 1800's with the number of historical publications growing in number. The CGP links its search results to depository library selection profiles. With this linking feature, users can locate the library nearest them that has a specific title in their collection. This feature also provides librarians an excellent referral tool. Direct access to online Federal publications is available from the CGP's bibliographic records through an embedded hyperlink, known as a persistent uniform resource locator (PURL). The PURL provides a direct link to the online title described in the cataloging record. GPO seeks new projects and partnerships that allow the scope of the CGP to grow and include more records for historical publications.

A recent enhancement to the CGP is the addition of MetaLib. You may simultaneously search GPO's main databases (CGP and FDsys). This federated search engine also allows users to search across 54 U.S. Federal Government databases retrieving reports, articles, and citations and link directly to resources available online.

28

Access to Archival Databases (AAD) System - NARA	Defense Technical Information Center (DTIC) - S&T Research: Public Technical Reports	Federal Reserve Board: International Finance Discussion Papers (IFDPs)	National Archives and Records Administration (NARA)	Patent and Trademark Office (USPTO) Patent Database
AGRICOLA Articles (NAL)	Department of Energy (DOE) Information Bridge	Federal Reserve Board: Reports to Congress	National Criminal Justice Reference Service Abstracts Database	PLANTS Database
AGRICOLA Books	Education Resources Information Center (ERIC)	Federal Reserve Board: Speeches and Testimony	National Environmental Publications Information Systems	PubMed
Archival Research Catalog (ARC) of the National Archives	Energy Citations Database (OSTI)	Federal Reserve Board: Staff Studies	National Institutes of Health (NIH)	THOMAS (Library of Congress)
Army Heritage Collection Online (AHCO) Digital Document System	Energy Information Administration (EIA)	Federal Reserve Board: Staff Studies	National Library of Medicine (NLM) Gateway	Treesearch -- Forest Service Research & Development
Army Heritage Collection Online (AHCO) Research Catalog	Environmental Health Perspectives	Federal Sector Appellate Decisions	National Technical Information Service (NTIS)	TRIS Online
AUL Index to Military Periodicals	Environmental Protection Agency (EPA) Catalog Search	GAO Reports and Testimony	National Transportation Library (NTL) Catalog	U.S. Army Center of Military History
CancerLit	EPA Publications and Newsletters	Geospatial One Stop (geodata.gov)	National Transportation Library (NTL) Digital Repository	USA.gov
Catalog of U.S. Government Publications (CGP)	EPA Scientific Inventory	Library of Congress (LOC)	National Transportation Library (NTL) - Integrated Search	USGS Library Catalog
Data.gov	Federal Digital System (FDsys)	MERLN Group Catalog	National Transportation Library (NTL) Transportation Websites	USGS Publications Warehouse
	Federal Reserve Board: Finance and Economic Discussion Series	NASA Technical Reports Server (NTRS)	Northern Prairie Wildlife Research Center (NPWRC) Publications	Water Resources of the United States

The FDLP maintains a Digitization Projects Registry. You can add your digitization projects to the Registry, avoid duplication by discovering what other organizations are digitizing, and locate possible partners for a collaborative project.

GPO collaborates with Federal libraries in the FLICC Preservation and Digitization Working Group and adheres to the standards for digitization as established by the membership of the Federal Agencies Digitization Guidelines Initiative. GPO is a member of the International Internet Preservation Consortium, a worldwide internet preservation alliance.

Federal agencies, departments, and offices publish vast numbers of online and tangible documents every year. As so many are published, not all documents are identified for inclusion in the FDLP. The FDLP encourages Federal depository librarians to help discover documents so that GPO can catalog these documents and make them available to the public through the CGP.

Report titles that are not in the CGP by sending an email to DocDiscovery@gpo.gov and provide brief bibliographic information (e.g., title, agency, date, URL, OCLC number).

Legislative Mandates

Title 44 of the U.S. Code contains laws governing public printing and documents. Chapter 19 specifically provides the authority for the establishment and operation of the FDLP. Among other things, this chapter gives the Superintendent of Documents responsibility for acquiring, classifying, and distributing to libraries and ensuring long-term permanent access of Federal Government information products. The U.S. Code and OMB Circular A-130 require Federal agencies to make all of their publications, in all formats, available to the Superintendent of Documents for distribution to depository libraries. Authority for the sales and cataloging and indexing programs is contained in Chapter 17 of Title 44. GPO began printing the Monthly Catalog of United States Government Publications (MOCAT) with the passage of the Printing Act of 1895. The CGP began as the online counterpart of the print MOCAT in the early 1990s. With Congress' approval, the print MOCAT ceased in December 2004 and the CGP took its place in law as the official catalog of all United States Federal Government publications.

In 1993, Congress passed the U.S. Government Printing Office Electronic Information Access Enhancement Act (Public Law 103-40), which expanded GPO's mission to provide electronic access to Federal electronic information. The GPO Access law is contained in Chapter 41. In June 1994, GPO launched *GPO Access* which provided online access to information from all three branches of the Federal Government for more than 15 years; it shut down in March 2012. The next generation of Government information online, the Federal Digital System (FDsys), replaces *GPO Access*.

FDLP Designation

Federal agency libraries eligible for depository status include:
• Libraries of major bureaus or divisions of Federal departments;
• Libraries of independent Federal agencies; and
• Libraries of service academies.
The Superintendent of Documents evaluates requests from Federal agencies seeking depository status. The evaluation will focus on such areas as commitment to serving the public; staff, space, and budget allocated to the depository collection and the number; and the scope, and character of the items selected. For more on the designation process, see the Designation Handbook for Federal Depository Libraries.

Federal Libraries in the FDLP

Since security in most Federal buildings is restricted in some manner, unplanned or unescorted access may be difficult to accommodate immediately. However, free public access is still a requirement for all depository libraries. Federal libraries may require the public to make arrangements in advance as well as to show identification, and/or to have an escort.

Users can find libraries in the FDLP in the Federal Depository Library Directory by searching for the various types of designations. In 2012, the FDLP included 54 Federal libraries in the executive, judicial, and legislatives branches (4 service academies, 12 court, and 38 Federal agency libraries).

V. Management in Federal Libraries

Libraries in the federal government offer management positions at various levels. Even a first federal job can include supervising employees and/or managing a unit. Job announcements advertised in the federal government include supervisory librarian positions and titles might be branch chief or division chief overseeing areas such as technical services, public services, electronic services or other units. Even postings for librarians in a one- or two-person library may require an individual to manage all of the activities in their library.

Management in federal Libraries follows the basic principles of administration seen in non-governmental libraries and business and encompasses the following major areas:

- ψ Agency Environment
- ψ Planning
- ψ Organizing
- ψ Leading
- ψ Controlling

Richard L. Daft defines management as "the attainment of organizational goals in an effective and efficient manner through planning, organizing, leading, and controlling organizational resources[1]." An effective federal government depends on innovative people who are willing to motivate and work with people at all levels to solve problems, develop solutions, create services, improve processes, and implement systems to meet and anticipate their customer's needs. There is a great deal of variety in federal government libraries, but what they all have in common is the requirement for effective and efficient managers and leaders who will add value to the organization.

Agency Environment

Before a new librarian can be an effective manager in a Federal agency, it is incumbent to learn the agency's vision, mission, and overall strategy for the next several years. This may mean reviewing federal laws, regulations, and other policies to understand the agency and how the librarian and the library play a part in the overall mission and direction of the agency. Begin with the agency's web site and learn of agency publications, products, and services. Discover the materials the library holds regarding the agency. Similar to conducting an environmental scan in library school for writing collection development policies, perform a scan for the agency library to gain a view of the external environment affecting the agency and the internal environment (culture, employees, management) that influence this agency or organization. The FEDLINK Competencies for Federal Librarians list the knowledge, skills, and abilities required for agency and organizational knowledge.

Planning

Planning involves developing goals and a means to accomplishing those goals in the library. Depending on the size of the library, planning could range from an informal process of brainstorming with staff to a formal strategic planning process resulting in a formal document or business plan. The first step is a mission statement—the organization's purpose and reason for being and a vision statement –ideally where the organization desires to be. (For more information on mission and vision statements goals, and objectives, see the management books listed in the references at the end of this chapter.) Even unit, branch, and division managers will often develop goals that align with the library and organization mission. Planning is fundamental and works best with sound decision-making techniques for developing a direction for the future.

Organizing

Organizing has to do with agency structure, the organization chart, chain of command, and division of labor. Military agencies, for example, tend to be very hierarchical in structure and a library could be a division within a directorate of the agency. The position of the library in a federal agency and its reporting chain may be very important to the level of resources, authority, credibility, and influence the library has overall. Understanding the big picture is important for new librarians/managers in federal libraries to be effective in communicating with stakeholders and customers. Within the library, managers today may design non-traditional models to allow for cross training, with an emphasis on electronic services, mobile services, and systems.

Leading

Leading has several components and all are important to achieving effective organizations. First, managers at all levels can be leaders in their organization and can help shape employee attitudes by bringing a positive approach and optimistic point of view to the agency. Studies show that attitudes arrive of three areas: thoughts, feelings, and behavior. Since cognitions or thoughts affect feelings and behavior, managers should be aware that influencing any one of these aspects could affect attitudes in the workplace. Job satisfaction and organizational commitment are important attitudes in the workplace and may contribute to outstanding performance; as a manager, seek creative ways to establish an environment to achieve this.

Emotional Intelligence (EQ) is now regarded as an important trait for leadership. New library managers may use self-development resources to strengthen emotional intelligence to better work with employees and leaders. Leadership style is also important for effective management and there are a variety of resources to help them develop appropriate leadership styles for different situations.

Leadership is the ability to influence people, and managers need this ability as much as other concrete skills to gain cooperation, enthusiasm, and results from employees. Outstanding leaders are able to motivate others, so it is vital to develop ideas for motivating staff.

Finally, leadership may mean leading teams rather than managing units. Federal agencies, like corporations, may accomplish objectives through teams. Teams may be set up formally as part of the organization's structure, or informally, to accomplish projects. Formal teams might consist of a supervisor and subordinates or personnel from across different horizontal levels in the organization. Informal teams, also known as self-directed teams, may call on a manager to lead or be part of one of these special purpose teams.

When leading a team, there are several important characteristics of a successful team. First, a leader must build trust among the team members. This may involve setting up icebreaker sessions and/or team building exercises. This is commonly referred to as forming the team. Next, the leader will promote healthy conflict, open-ended discussion, and problem solving among members so that individuals feel comfortable expressing opinions. When the team has trust, commitment will occur and people will buy into the decisions and goals of the team. With commitment and trust will also come accountability, so that members hold one another accountable--rather than a manager--for success. Finally, building the team will also promote a results-oriented atmosphere, and, this will help achieve success collectively. Books on leading teams as well as opportunities for training exist to help with this challenge; such information will lead to developing the five stages of a team:

- ψ Forming: Orientation phase where the leader helps with breaking the ice and facilitating social interaction among members

- ψ Storming: Conflict stage where there is disagreement, conflict, jockeying for position, and the leader tries to encourage discussion, participation, and open up the meeting to differences of opinion

- ψ Norming: Orderly phase where members now have a team focus and the leader helps everyone to retain group cohesion and know their roles, norms, and values

- ψ Performing: Cooperative stage where the team is working together toward the objective of the project and the leader facilitates the end goal

- ψ Adjourning: End phase where the project is finished and the leader attempts to bring some closure to the entire team effort and deal with the emotion of disbanding the team.

Running an effective team is similar to running an effective meeting. There are many resources with tips on running an effective meeting. Preparation is paramount and defining the purpose of the meeting, inviting the right people, and preparing an agenda that identifies the expected outcomes streamline meeting planning. Meetings need to begin and end on time. Be sure to restate the purpose and review the agenda, establish ground rules for discussion, create involvement from all members, and keep the meeting moving along. Some meetings may require a timekeeper and someone to take meeting minutes. At the end of the meeting, summarize the discussion and any tasks assigned. Send minutes out promptly with agreed upon tasks.

Controlling

Controlling covers many areas in organizations such as budgeting, employee performance, and organizational evaluation such as total quality management or benchmarking. Federal supervisors often deal with control issues related to work processes, financial resources, employee behavior, systems, and evaluation. Daft defines organizational control as "the systematic process of regulating organizational activities to make them consistent with the expectations established in plans, targets, and standards performance." [2]

Supervisors can be responsible for a budget for a unit, branch, division, or for the whole library. This often involves planning for the next fiscal year, expending and monitoring funds for the current fiscal year, and year-end reporting. A library director will be responsible for the budget, but may share parts of the control process with supervisors or team leaders. It is also common to see libraries produce business plans which lay out the financial picture of the library and include future planning. The Defense Acquisition University and the Graduate School USA both offer courses on the federal budgeting process.

Another aspect of control is evaluation of library functions and processes. Since the 1980s there have been a number of philosophies on how best to evaluate the agency; these include total quality management (TQM), quality circles, benchmarking, lean six sigma, continuous improvement, service standards, and balanced scorecard. Each agency may have adopted one or more of these tools to assess its results, progress, or success.

Technology has allowed all libraries to perform better selection, organize materials and resources, provide access, build repositories, and disseminate information inside and outside of the government. Since technology is constantly evolving, librarians must adapt to changing conditions and trends in the market place and in government transformation to keep up with the new solutions and business processes. Social media can assists libraries in marketing, advertising library services and communicating with library stakeholders. While some restrictions exist in federal agencies, there are many great opportunities to apply new technologies to enhance services and programs in libraries.

Supervision

The Office of Personnel Management (OPM) offers supervisors resources under the Resources for HR practitioners link. Topics include human capital, hiring authorities, and classification and qualifications. Under classification and qualifications, you will find information and resources to develop job descriptions and classify jobs into the appropriate series and level for the work that you need performed:

- ψ Classifying General Schedule Positions

- ψ Handbook of Occupational Groups and Families

- ψ General Schedule Qualification Policies

- ψ General Schedule Qualification Standards

At OPM, you will find information to help you learn about Federal laws regarding types of leave including family medical leave, employee assistance programs, employee relations, diversity, accommodations for persons with disabilities and other human resources' topics. As you gain experience in supervision, you can seek out workshops to build your skills in interviewing, selecting, hiring, coaching, motivating, creating individual development plans, evaluating, disciplining, resolving conflicts, stress management, and rewarding employees—keeping in mind the most important part of the human capital process is hiring the right person for what you need in the first place and then developing that person so that he/she becomes a valuable asset for your organization.

References

The following reference list offers information on many aspects of supervision and management, leadership development, change management, and personal growth for a federal library and information career.

Blanchard, K., and Johnson S. (2003) *The .01 minute manager.* New York: HarperCollins. (management basics)

Blanchard, K., Hoekstra, J., & Zigarmi, P. (2009) *Who killed change?* New York: HarperCollins. (change management)

Brounstein, M., Donaldson, M. C., Economy, P., Elkin, A., Fox, S. Johnson, K....Ziglar, Zig. (2010). *Thriving in the workplace: All-in-one for dummies.* New York: Wiley. (leadership and management)

Buckingham, M. & Coffman, C. (1999). *First, break all the rules: What the world's greatest managers do differently.* New York: Simon & Schuster. (leadership and management)

Burns, J. M. (2010) *Leadership.* New York: Harper. (classic leadership text)

Caba, S. (2013). *Complete idiot's guide to leadership: fast-track.* New York: Penguin. (short leadership tips)

Covert, J. & Sattersten, T. (2011). *The 100 best business books of all time: What they say, why they matter, and how they can help you.* New York: Penguin. (Bibliographic essays)

Covey, S. R. (2004). *The 7 habits of highly effective people: Restoring the character ethic.* New York: Free Press. (personal organization and effectiveness)

Covery, S.R. (2004). *The 8th habit: From effectiveness to greatness.* New York: Free Press. (motivating others)

Deming, W. E. (2000). *Out of the crisis.* Boston: MIT Press. (quality movement)

Drucker, P. F. (2008). *The essential Drucker: The best sixty years of Peter Drucker's essential writings on management.* New York: HarperCollins. (management and leadership)

Goldstein, D., Boyatzis, R., & McKee, A. (2013). *Primal leadership: Unleashing the power of emotional intelligence.* Boston, Harvard Review Press. (EQ)

Gordon, J. (2007). *The energy bus: 10 rules to fuel your life, work, and team with positive energy.* New York: Wiley. (team building)

Heath, C. & Heath, D. (2010) *Switch: how to change things when change is hard.* New York: Broadway Books. (transformative change)

Heller, R. & Hindle, T. (2008). *DK essential manager's manual.* New York: DK (management)

Hunsaker, P. & Alessandra, T. (2008). *The new art of managing people.* Rev. New York: Free Press. (management)

Johnson, S. (1998). *Who moved my cheese?* New York: G. P. Putnam (personal motivation)

Karsh, B. & Templin, C. (2013). *A millenial's guide to rewriting the rules of management.* New York: AMACOM. (managing generations in the workplace)

Kotter, J. P. (2012). *Leading change.* Boston: Harvard Business Review. (change management)

Kotter, J. P. & Rathgeber, H. (2005). Our *iceberg is melting: changing and succeeding under any conditions.* New York: St. Martin's Press. (change management)

Kouzes, J. M., and Posner, B. Z. (2012). *The leadership challenge: how to make extraordinary things happen in organizations.* 5th ed. San Francisco: Jossey-Bass. (leadership)

Kouzes, J. M. & Posner, B. Z. (2008). *The leadership challenge.* San Francisco: Jossey-Bass. (leadership)

Lencioni, P. (2002). *The five dysfunctions of a team: A leadership fable.* San Francisco: Jossey-Bass. (teams and team building)

Lundin, S. C., Paul, H. & Christensen, J. (2000). *Fish: A proven way to boost morale and improve results.* New York: Hyperion. (performance)

Malhotra, D. (2013). *I moved your cheese: For those who refuse to live as mice in someone else's maze.* San Francisco: Berrett-Koehler. (personal motivation)

Marquet, L. D. (2012). *Turn the ship around: A true story of turning followers into leaders.* New York: Portfolio/Penguin. (empowering leadership)

Maxwell, J. C. (2007). *The 21 irrefutable laws of leadership: Follow them and people will follow you.* Nashville: Thomas Nelson. (leadership)

Nelson, B. & Economy, P. (2010). *Managing for dummies.* 3rd ed. New York: Wiley. (management)

Feffer, J. & Sutton, R. I. (2000). *The knowing-doing gap: how smart companies turn knowledge into action.* Boston: Harvard Business School Press. (classic management)

Rath, T. & Conche, B. (2008). *Strengths based leadership: Great leaders, teams, and why people follow.* New York: Gallup Press. (strengths)

Scholtes, P. R. , Joiner, B. L., & Streibel, B. (2003). *The team handbook.* 3rd ed. Oriel. (teams and team building)

Tracy, B. & Chee, P. (2013). *12 disciplines of leadership excellence: How leaders achieve sustainable high performance.* New York: McGraw-Hill. (leadership)

VI. FEDLINK

About FEDLINK

The Federal Library and Information Network (FEDLINK) is an organization of federal agencies working together to achieve optimum use of the resources and facilities of federal libraries and information centers by promoting common services, coordinating and sharing available resources, and providing continuing professional education for federal library and information staff. FEDLINK serves as a forum for discussion of the policies, programs, procedures, and technologies that affect federal libraries and the information services they provide to their agencies, to the Congress, the federal courts and the American people.

Originally established by the Librarian of Congress in 1963 as the Federal Library Committee (later the Federal Library and Information Center Committee or "FLICC"), FEDLINK continues in recognition of the need for cooperation and concerted action within the community of federal libraries and information centers in the 21st century. In 2001, the Congress established a statutory revolving fund under 2 U.S.C. § 182c to support FEDLINK interagency procurement and library support efforts.

The FEDLINK Bylaws define the mission, membership and governing structure. FEDLINK is composed of the directors of the national libraries: the Library of Congress, National Library of Medicine, the National Agricultural Library, the National Library of Education, and the National Transportation Library; representatives of cabinet-level executive departments; legislative, judicial, and independent federal agencies, and is chaired by the Librarian of Congress.

The mission of FEDLINK is to achieve better use of federal library and information resources; to provide the most cost-effective and efficient mechanism for procuring necessary services and materials for federal libraries and information centers; to serve as a forum for discussion of federal library and information policies, programs and procedures; and to help inform Congress, federal agencies and others concerned with libraries and information centers. FEDLINK coordinates cooperative activities and services among federal libraries and information centers. It serves as a forum for federal librarians and information professionals to interact, consider, and make recommendations through the Librarian of Congress concerning issues and policies that affect federal libraries and information centers, needs and priorities in providing information services to the federal government and to the nation at large, and efficient and cost-effective use of federal library and information resources and services. FEDLINK encourages advances in (a) improved access to information, (b) research and development in the application of new information technologies, (c) improvements in management of federal libraries and information centers, (d) stewardship and preservation of federal information resources, and (e) relevant educational opportunities.

FEDLINK Advisory Board (FAB)

The FEDLINK Advisory Board (FAB) comprises thirteen voting members: the Chair, who serves ex officio, and twelve individuals appointed by the Chair – nine elected by the FEDLINK membership and three selected by the Chair. The FEDLINK Executive Director serves as an ex-officio, nonvoting member of the FAB.

The FAB proposes program policies, objectives and plans, recommend an annual budget, establishes FEDLINK committees, working groups and advisory councils, apprises the federal library community of issues of general interest and of those related to FEDLINK programs, services, policies or objectives and provide advice, policy guidance, and oversight to the FEDLINK program.

FEDLINK Committees, Working Groups, Advisory Boards

Volunteers from federal libraries and information centers lend their expertise to the entire federal information community by serving on FEDLINK Working Groups, which actively support a wide range of FEDLINK programs. Each group focuses on an area of importance to federal librarians and information specialists, including information policy issues, information technology, education, preservation, human resources, and cooperative endeavors. Standing working groups meet regularly, while ad hoc working groups are formed to discuss special issues of interest.

FEDLINK has standing working groups (Budget & Finance, Policy, Nominating, Membership and Governance, Education, and Survey) and ad hoc working groups (Awards, FEDGrey - Grey Literature, Information Technology, Human Resources, Library Technicians, New Federal Librarians (NewFeds), and Preservation).

From time to time advisory councils form for special projects (i.e., provide advice to a federal library program manager charged with implementing reorganization of their agency's library services). The working groups, committees and councils are comprised of staff from the federal library and information center community. To volunteer to serve on a Working Group or obtain more information regarding current projects and activities of a specific working group, committee or council, call the FLICC Publications and Education Office at (202) 707-4820 or email fliccfpe@loc.gov.

FEDLINK's Business Model

As federal agencies experience budget constraints and reduced spending, the need increases for an efficient and effective centralized operation such as FEDLINK. FEDLINK streamlines procurement for federal agencies in all three branches of government by establishing contracts for commercial information resources, publications in all formats and other support services for federal libraries and information programs. FEDLINK reduces the burden on agency administrative staff by establishing a simplified, centralized method for procuring information services and providing financial management services. FEDLINK has successfully provided these services to more than 1,000 government units for more than 25 years. Through FEDLINK, agencies have access to an expanded supplier base for increased competition, an improved payment process, and knowledgeable and experienced federal staff who can assist with steps in the procurement process.

FEDLINK offers procurement and financial/educational support on a fee-for-service basis. The FEDLINK program is de-signed to help federal librarians, contracting officers, and finance staff save time, effort, and money when buying and using library and information services (online systems, CD-ROMs, books, and periodicals). Through its FEDLINK program, the Library of Congress shares its expertise in library and information services and consolidates the buying power of federal agencies. Detailed information about service options, eligibility, and fees are available through the Member Financial Services section of the FLICC Web site.

Discounts earned by FEDLINK group procurement and the increased reporting and budget control FEDLINK provides directly benefit agency libraries, information centers, and other federal offices. In addition to its procurement effort, FEDLINK provides accounting support to members. Agencies transfer dollars to FEDLINK via interagency agreements and work with FEDLINK's specialists to place orders following federal acquisitions regulations for competition, etc. This method of using FEDLINK contracts is called "Transfer Pay." Alternatively, most FEDLINK contracts can be used by agencies to place their own orders directly with the vendors and pay their own invoices. However, more cost avoidance and processing efficiency is achieved by use of Transfer Pay.

The Federal Sourcing Strategy

The Office of Management and Budget (OMB) has designated FEDLINK as the lead agent for information resources under the Federal Strategic Services Initiative (FSSI). In this role, FEDLINK will acquire information products and services—such as online databases, subscriptions, books, maps and newspapers—on behalf of federal agencies that opt into the program. This acquisitions service alone could potentially save hundreds of millions of dollars and increase access to information resources for the benefit of the American people.

FEDLINK already serves as a centralized manager of information products and services acquisitions on behalf of more than 90 federal agencies and bureaus throughout all branches of the government. By expanding services through strategic sourcing, FEDLINK could potentially save the government between $140 million and $555 million over the next four years, depending on participation, according to a report by the Federal Research Division (FRD) at the Library of Congress.

Beginning in FY2014, new contracts for information retrieval services (e.g., databases and other electronic publications) will meet FSSI requirements and provide more opportunities and support for agencies to consolidate orders, gain deeper discounts and avoid administrative costs. FEDLINK formed commodity councils in two subject areas, legal and Science/Technology/Engineering/Math (STEM), to bring together subject matter experts to advise them on opportunities and challenges in those areas. Legal and STEM were selected as the areas where the most federal dollars are spent obtaining electronic access to commercially published information.

Authority

Statutory Authority

Section 103 of P.L. 106-481 (2 U.S.C. 182c) establishes FEDLINK as a revolving fund, effective Fiscal Year 2002. The law authorizes the FEDLINK revolving fund to provide "the procurement of commercial information services, publications in any format, and library support services, ...related accounting services,...related education, information and support services" to federal offices and to other organizations entitled to use federal sources of supply (Subpart (f)(1)). This work is conducted under interagency agreements (IAGs) between LC and FEDLINK "member" agencies.

Procurement Authority

The Library of Congress Contracts and Logistics Services (LC/C&M) conducts FEDLINK procurement. It is Library of Congress policy to follow the FAR in its own contracting, even though technically, as a Legislative branch agency, LC is not subject to that regulation. For the FEDLINK program, LC follows the FAR as a service to FEDLINK members, most of whom are Executive agencies subject to the FAR. FEDLINK contractual vehicles are normally basic ordering agreements (BOAs), pursuant to 48 C.F.R. § 16.7. They are administered by LC contracting officers with support from FEDLINK librarians who serve as contracting officers' representatives (CORs).

Advance Payment

Because FEDLINK has revolving fund authority, FEDLINK customers can advance funds to pay for products and services.

Business Rules for Intragovernmental Exchange Transactions

FEDLINK is in procedural compliance with the requirements of the Office of Management and Budget's (OMB) Business Rules for Intragovernmental Exchange Transactions (Office of Management and Budget (Memorandum # M-03-01).

Eligibility
Federal Agencies

LC is authorized to provide FEDLINK services to other federal agencies and to organizations that are authorized to use federal sources of supply. Accordingly, FEDLINK services are available to any library, information center, or other activity (such as offices of general counsel, procurement units, information resource management departments, laboratories, etc.) within the executive, legislative, or judicial branches of the United States federal government, including activities within all branches of the U.S. armed forces, and the District of Columbia.

Federal Contractors or Other Non-Governmental Entities

In some cases, non-governmental entities may use FEDLINK services. Contractors working for federal agencies, for example, may be authorized to use government supply sources and may therefore be eligible to use FEDLINK. The LC General Counsel has determined that FEDLINK cannot assume that a contractor or other non-governmental entity who registers for the program is eligible. LC must inquire by what authority the request to use FEDLINK is made.

Therefore, if an organization is a contractor or other entity authorized to use government supply sources by 48 C.F.R. § 51 and FAR 51.102, the agency's administrator or another authorized federal official must send a letter to the FLICC Executive Director specifying a contractor's status enables it to use FEDLINK.

FEDLINK Acquisitions

FEDLINK uses a four-step acquisitions model:
- ψ simplified acquisition of commercial information services and products, favored customer pricing, additional favorable terms and discount and volume pricing for services and acquisitions
- ψ elimination of the high cost of duplicating contracting cycles and the cost associated with individual orders
- ψ economies of scale from centralized examination, invoice payments and accounting
- ψ controlled budgeting and spending based on service usage and payment trend.

FEDLINK Products & Services

FEDLINK offers information services from a variety of vendors including
- ψ Information Retrieval
- ψ Book Jobbers
- ψ Serial Subscription Agents
- ψ Preservation/Digital Archiving Digitization
- ψ Technical Processing/Cataloging
- ψ Integrated Library Systems
- ψ Interlibrary Loan/Copyright
- ψ Staffing
- ψ Other Specialized Library Support Services/Bibliographic Utilities

FEDLINK Vendors

FEDLINK vendors offer a variety of commercial information services. Over 80 companies offer access to content online under the information retrieval contracts. Document delivery services quickly locate, acquire, and deliver individual documents, including journal articles, technical reports, dissertations, theses, and other published and unpublished materials in print or electronic format.

For other publications acquisition, FEDLINK book jobbers or wholesalers provide a central channel for acquiring monographs, eliminating the need for agencies to deal directly with thousands of individual publishers or to order from local bookstores. Serials subscription agents also improve the management of agency journal collections (magazines, periodicals, newspapers, etc.) by consolidating orders and renewals for hundreds of thousands of journal titles. They provide additional services to help libraries manage online and print subscriptions such as processing claims and maintaining links.

Among FEDLINK's library support services are preservation, conservation and digitization of collections, and software to manage access to digital objects. Web-based online language courseware is available. Several companies that offer specialized services are also available, such as OCLC, Outsell, the Copyright Clearance Center, and fee payment for interlibrary loans. FEDLINK has assisted libraries in their procurement of integrated library systems, cataloging and staffing.

FEDLINK Education Program

Supported by the volunteer efforts of the FEDLINK Education Working Group, FEDLINK offers a wide range of educational opportunities for federal librarians, information specialists and technical staff. Event descriptions and registration are both available online. From casual brown bag lunches where librarians can ask questions of their colleagues on topics such as Web page development and contract administration, to the popular Great Escapes tours of major federal collections, FLICC educational programs provide unique opportunities for federal information personnel to learn from each other and share ideas about providing better information service.

FEDLINK programs have covered copyright law for librarians and computer professionals, preservation of non-book materials, end-user training, MARC format integration, government information on the Internet, and the application of technology to library resources and operations.

The crowning event in FLICC's educational year are two semiannual FEDLINK Expositions. These expos address a broad topic of emerging importance to the federal information community and provides an opportunity for the exchange of ideas among the public, private, and nonprofit sectors.

For the latest information on FEDLINK programs, training and events, view the Upcoming Events section of the main FEDLINK Webpage.

FEDLINK Web Site

FEDLINK's Web site offers descriptions of FEDLINK initiatives, educational programs, publications, and federal library issues; links to FEDLINK member and contracting services; secure electronic fiscal reporting on daily account balances, statement detail, and usage data.

Topic areas include
- ψ Publications
- ψ Meeting Announcements
- ψ Education & Training
- ψ FEDLINK Expositions & Awards
- ψ FEDLINK Photo Album
- ψ Federal Library Resources
- ψ Contracting/Vendor Products & Services
- ψ Account Management
- ψ Information for Vendors

FEDLINK also offers two listservs, organized by specific areas of expertise or interest and keep members informed while offering them networking and discussion opportunities.

FEDLIB-- The Federal Librarians Discussion List is a moderated mailing list for the staff of libraries and information centers in the federal government, although other subscribers are welcome. FEDLINK moderates discussions of FEDLINK news and meeting announcements, federal library management, the position of the federal library within the larger agency, and ideas and suggestions about the FLICC/ FEDLINK program and its services to federal libraries.

FEDREF-L -- The Federal Reference Librarians Discussion List is a moderated list for reference librarians in the federal government, although other subscribers are welcome. Discussions cover issues affecting the whole range of federal library public services including reference, interlibrary loan, and circulation.

Contact FEDLINK

Call the FEDLINK Fiscal Hotline at (202) 707-4900 to join more than 1,000 other federal libraries and information centers that save time and money through FEDLINK. For more information, visit the FEDLINK Web page.

VII. Copyright Management in the Federal Library or Information Center

As information managers for publicly supported institutions, federal librarians procure published materials in a variety of formats for federal employees and the public to perform their research and enhance their work. Generally, federal libraries do not own rights in the materials in their collection. Because most of these are protected by copyright, federal librarians must educate agency managers, staff, and the public they serve about copyright responsibilities. The following guidelines serve as a framework for providing direction regarding the use, reproduction, and distribution of library materials in federal libraries and information centers.

What is Copyright?

The U.S. Constitution, Article 1, Section 8, provides that "The Congress shall have power...To promote the progress of Science and Useful Arts, by Securing for Limited Times to Authors and Inventors the exclusive right to their respective Writings and Discoveries." The U.S. Copyright Office Circular 1, COPYRIGHT BASICS, states that "Copyright is a form of protection provided by the laws of the United States to the authors of "original works of authorship" including literary, dramatic, musical, artistic, and certain other intellectual works." Under the revised and amended Copyright Act of 1976 (17 USC 106 and 106A), creators have the exclusive rights to: 1) reproduce; 2) distribute 3) make derivatives 4) publicly perform 5) publicly display and 6) moral attribution. This protection automatically extends to published or unpublished "original works of authorship fixed in any tangible medium of expression, now known or later developed, from which they can be perceived, reproduced, or otherwise communicated, either directly or with the aid of a machine or device." (17 USC 101).

Works Protected by Copyright:

- ψ Books
- ψ Periodicals
- ψ Newspapers
- ψ Databases
- ψ Photographs
- ψ Art
- ψ Music
- ψ Web Sites
- ψ Microform
- ψ Films
- ψ Videotapes

Works Not Protected:

Several categories of material are generally not eligible for federal copyright protection. These include among others:

- ψ Works that have not been fixed in a tangible form of expression, (i.e., choreographic works that have not been scored or recorded, or improvisational speeches or performances that have not been written or recorded).
- ψ Titles, names, short phrases, and slogans; familiar symbols or designs; mere variations of typographic ornamentation, lettering, or coloring; mere listings of ingredients or contents. Some of these may be protected under trademarks or servicemarks.

- ψ Ideas, procedures, methods, systems, processes, concepts, principles, discoveries, or devices, as distinguished from a description, explanation, or illustration. These may be protected under patents or trade secrets.
- ψ Works consisting entirely of information that is common property and containing no original authorship (for example: standard calendars, height and weight charts, tape measures and rulers, and lists or tables taken from public documents or other common sources). Only the expression of the idea is eligible for copyright.

Works in the Public Domain

Works in the public domain may be used by anyone, anywhere, anytime without permission, license or royalty payment. They are publicly available and are not owned or protected by copyright. Be cautioned that "public domain" is not synonymous and should not be confused or used interchangeably to mean "free access," "publicly available," or in government parlance, "public release." For example, the Internet version of the Washington Post is free access and publicly available, but protected by copyright. Works in the public domain include

- ψ Works on which the copyright owner abandons copyright.
- ψ Works on which the statutory copyright protection expires. The Sonny Bono

Copyright Term Extension Act (PL 105-298, 27 Oct 98) extended the term for published works to the life of the author plus 70 years. Published corporate works are protected for 95 years from the date of publication. However, works published prior to 1923 are now in the public domain. For more detailed information, see the U.S. Copyright Office Circular 15, Renewal of Copyright; Circular 15a, Duration of Copyright; and Circular 15t, Extension of Copyright Terms.

Works of the U.S. Government

People often presume that if information comes from a U.S. Government source then it is in the "public domain." Only "Government Works" created entirely by an officer or employee of the United States Government as part of that person's official duties are not protected by copyright in United States (17 USC 105).

- ψ Contractors and grantees are not considered Government employees. Generally they hold copyright to works they produce for the Government and grant the Government an irrevocable, worldwide, nonexclusive, royalty-free license to "use, modify, reproduce, release, perform, display or disclose" government contracted works within the government without restriction and to allow others to do so for U.S. Government purposes. See CENDI Frequently Asked Questions about Copyright, Chapter 4, for additional guidance.
- ψ Also note, a privately created work (e.g. quote, photograph, chart, drawing, etc.) used with permission in a U.S. Government work does not place the private work in the public domain.
- ψ Therefore, it is important to read the permissions and copyright notices on U.S. Government publications and Web sites. Many Government agencies follow the practice of providing notice for material that is copyrighted and not for that in the public domain. For additional information see "Digital Rights, Copyright, Trademark, and Patent".

Limitations on Exclusive Rights of Authors

Fair Use Doctrine

To balance the rights of intellectual property owners with the need for using materials protected by copyright "to promote the progress of science and useful arts," the doctrine of Fair Use evolved through a number of court decisions and was codified in Section 107 of the Copyright Act.

Under certain circumstances, it allows the reproduction and use of works protected by copyright without the express consent of the copyright owners. Some examples of "fair use" purposes are criticism, comment, news reporting, teaching, scholarship and research. Additionally, there are four factors to consider together in the legal analysis; these are

1. the purpose and character of the use, including whether such use is of a commercial nature or is for nonprofit commercial purposes.
2. the nature of the copyrighted work.
3. the effect of the use upon the potential market value for or value of the copyrighted work.
4. the effect of the use upon the potential market for or value of the copyrighted work

While the Government may rely on fair use, the use of materials by the Government is not automatically a fair use. For an authoritative discussion, see: U.S. Department of Justice Opinion, Government Reproduction of Copyrighted Materials and Fair Use, April 30, 1999.

Library Exemptions

There are no special policies that apply to Government libraries and archives. However, under 17 USC 108, all libraries and archives are provided special rights with respect to study, research, interlibrary loan, archiving and preservation. See Copyright Office Circular 21: Reproductions of Copyrighted Works by Educators and Librarians for basic information on some of the most important provisions.

Library Reproduction and Distribution:

17 USC 108(a) states that "it is not an infringement of copyright for a library or archives, or any of its employees acting within the scope of their employment, to reproduce no more than one copy or phonorecord of a work, or to distribute such copy or phonorecord, under the conditions specified by this section, if the-

ψ   reproduction or distribution is made without any purpose of direct or indirect commercial advantage;
ψ   collections of the library or archives are (i) open to the public, or (ii) available not only to researchers affiliated with the library or archives or with the institution of which it is a part, but also to other persons doing research in a specialized field; and
ψ   reproduction or distribution of the work includes a notice of copyright..."

Interlibrary Loan and Document Delivery

Additional guidelines for library photocopying and interlibrary loan are provided in the National Commission on New Technological Uses of Copyright Works (CONTU) Guidelines on Photocopying under Interlibrary Loan Arrangements. These provide that

ψ   During a calendar year, a library may borrow five articles from a periodical title newer than five years old.
ψ   All interlibrary loan requests must bear a copyright notice.

The requesting library must keep borrowing records for three calendar years. Exceptions to this "Rule of Five" include when the title is on order, that issue is missing, the item is at the bindery, or the issue was damaged or not available.

The alternatives include borrowing the entire volume or issue, using a document delivery or full text service, obtaining permission from the copyright holder directly or joining a copyright clearing-house. Libraries that choose not to subscribe to such a service may simply keep track of their borrowing and lending habits and stop borrowing when their need necessitates purchasing the title directly. Most document delivery services factor the cost of copyright permissions into their fee. For a list of service providers, see Document Delivery Suppliers compiled by Jean Shipman, Tompkins-McCaw Library for the Health Sciences, VCU Libraries, Virginia Commonwealth University.

Library Archiving and Preservation

The Digital Millennium Copyright Act amended 17 USC 108 and covers making both digital and non-digital copies for library archiving and preservation. It permits the creation of three copies only if the library or archives has, after reasonable effort, determined that an unused replacement cannot be obtained at a reasonable price. These copies may not be distributed to the public outside the premises of the library or archive. The material may also be converted to a new format for preservation of access.

Electronic Publications

Purchased and Licensed Publications

In the paper environment, the rights and responsibilities of the purchaser and the producer are addressed by copyright law, fair use, and the " first sale" doctrine. However, in the digital environment, these are negotiated through contractual agreements and licenses. The terms of these agreements usually allow viewing materials and making reasonable copies for personal or agency use. Most specifically forbid:
> 1. Substantial or systematic reproduction
> 2. Systematic supply or distribution to non-authorized users.

It is important to critically read and negotiate license agreements for databases, e-books, and electronic journals or other subscription products. For further discussion and guidance, see the FEDLINK Video Presentation Licensing Electronic Publications for Use in a Federal Agency, CENDI's License Agreements for Electronic Products and Services: Frequently Asked Questions, and the National Library of Medicine Policy on Acquiring Copyrighted Material in Electronic Format.

Internet Free Access Publications

The Internet is another form of publishing; therefore, copyright applies to Web sites, e-mail messages, Web-based music, etc. Simply because the Internet provides easy access to the information does not mean that the information is in the public domain or is available without limitations. Works protected by copyright found on the Internet should be treated the same as copyright protected works found in other media.

An alternative to copying material found on the Internet is to link to it. "Hyperlinking does not itself involve a violation of the Copyright Act (whatever it may do for other claims) since no copying is involved." (Ticketmaster vs. Tickets.com (2000)). However, look before you link. Many organizations post terms and conditions and even how-to instructions on their websites; these are usually found under the headings of "Copyright", "Legal Notices", or "About Us". Be aware of other legal issues and prohibitions such as framing, misappropriation, passing off, and trademark infringement.

Three Ways of Working with Copyright Issues in a Federal Library

There are a variety of sources of information on copyright issues, but as a rule of thumb, every federal library or information center can:

- ψ Develop and implement a copyright policy. For example, see The Library of Congress About Copyright and Collections.
- ψ Be proactive in informing and educating users about copyright. Take an inventory of all materials protected by copyright, regardless of format, to determine whether there is any risk of copyright infringement. For example, an inventory of print or electronic subscriptions, along with an assessment of user demand for those materials, will disclose the potential for copyright infringement. Publicize your findings and policies; for example see the National Agriculture Library NAL Copyright Statement and Smithsonian Institution Libraries Terms of Use.
- ψ In accordance with 17 USC 108, display a photocopy warning notice near unsupervised photocopying equipment to alert users that reproducing copyright-protected material is subject to the Copyright Laws of the United States. Discourage photocopying the entire contents of publications, especially newsletters, journals, and books, regardless of format. See Unsupervised Copying Equipment, Copyright Advisory Office of Columbia University, Kenneth D. Crews, director.

Copyright References for Librarians

Articles/Books

Crews, Kenneth D. Copyright Essentials for Librarians and Educators. Chicago, IL: American Library Association, 2012. 208 pp.

Gasaway, Laura N., "Copyright Questions and Answers for Information Professionals," Purdue University Press, 2013, 284 pp.

Stim, Richard, "Getting Permission: How to License & Clear Copyrighted Materials Online & Off," 4th Edition, Nolo, October 2010, 424 pp.

Web Sites for Additional Information

- ψ US Copyright Office
- ψ CENDI Frequently Asked Questions about Copyright
- ψ Consortium for Educational Technology in University Systems (CETUS). Fair Use and Higher Education: A Statement of Principle – The Need to Address Fair Use
- ψ Copyright Clearance Center
- ψ Library of Congress. Federal Library & Information Network (FEDLINK) Copyright and Licensing resources
- ψ Stanford University Libraries Copyright and Fair Use
- ψ University of Texas System
- ψ University System of Georgia

VIII. Resources

This chapter is a sampling of available resources relevant to the field of federal librarianship and is not meant to be a comprehensive collection.   Included below are many free resources. Browse or use the topic links below to locate specific information.

Topics

Accessibility | Copyright | Digitization and Preservation | Directories | Executive Branch | Federal Depository Library Program | FEDLINK | Interlibrary Loan | Intelligence Resources | Judicial Branch | Legislative Branch | Management | Maps & Plans | Medical Resources | Military Resources | Professional Organizations | Professional Reading and Discussion Lists | Scientific and Technical Information | Standards and Best Practices | Statistics and Datasets | Technology

Accessibility

ALA Library Services for People with Disabilities Policy - http://www.ala.org/ala/mgrps/divs/ascla/asclaissues/libraryservices.cfm

Americans with Disabilities (ADA) National Network - http://www.adata.org/Static/Home.aspx

Applicants with Disabilities – http://www.opm.gov/disability/peoplewithdisabilities.asp

Assistive Technology (also known as Adaptive Technology) – http://www.section508.gov

Federal Disability Government Website – http://www.disability.gov

National Library Services for the Blind – http://www.loc.gov/nls

U.S. Equal Employment Opportunity Commission – http://www.eeoc.gov

USA Jobs Individuals with Disabilities – https://help.usajobs.gov/index.php/Individuals_with_Disabilities

Copyright

Copyright Crash Course – http://copyright.lib.utexas.edu

Digital Copyright Slider – http://www.librarycopyright.net/digitalslider - This is an interactive and preliminary estimator of public domain, but current Copyright.gov resources are more authoritative.

US Copyright Term and the Public Domain - http://copyright.cornell.edu/resources/publicdomain.cfm - This is a more detailed estimator of public domain, but current Copyright.gov resources are more authoritative.

Frequently Asked Questions About Copyright: Issues Affecting the U.S. Government (CENDI) – http://www.cendi.gov/publications/04-8copyright.html - This is a more detailed estimator of public domain, but current Copyright.gov resources are more authoritative.

United States Copyright Office – http://www.copyright.gov - Copyright research methods, circulars, and public domain information can be found through this site. Please note that all the information within is periodically updated.

Directory of Open Access Journals (DOAJ) – http://www.doaj.org

Directory of Open Access Repositories (OpenDOAR) – http://www.opendoar.org

Scholarly Publishing & Academic Resources Coalition (SPARC) - http://www.arl.org/sparc - Developed by the Association of Research Libraries, SPARC is an international alliance of academic and research libraries that promotes open access publishing.

Digitization and Preservation

Digital Preservation - http://www.digitalpreservation.gov - Home of the National Digital Stewardship Alliance, Digital Preservation Outreach and Education and the National Digital Information Infrastructure and Preservation Program

Federal Agencies Digitization Guidelines Initiative (FADGI) - http://www.digitizationguidelines.gov

Library of Congress Preservation Directorate - http://www.loc.gov/preserv

National Archives and Records Preservation - http://www.archives.gov/preservation

National Digital Information Infrastructure & Preservation Program (NDIIPP) - http://www.digitalpreservation.gov

Directories

Biographical Directory of the U.S. Congress (1874 – present) - http://bioguide.congress.gov/biosearch/biosearch.asp

Embassies, consulates and diplomatic missions of the U.S. government - http://www.usembassy.gov

Federal Library Directory – http://viewshare.org/views/FRD/directory -
From the Federal Research Division of the Library of Congress and FEDLINK (This list and interactive GIS map directory of Federal Libraries must be viewed with Mozilla Firefox.)

Federal Agency Directories-
Alphabetical - http://www.usa.gov/directory/federal/index.shtml
Hierarchical - http://www.lib.lsu.edu/gov/index.html

Government and Public Libraries – http://www.usa.gov/Topics/Reference_Shelf/Libraries.shtml

Members of Congress – http://congress.gov/members

United States Government Manual – http://www.usgovernmentmanual.gov - Official handbook of the federal government

Executive Branch

Federal eRulemaking portal - http://www.regulations.gov

FedWorld Information Network - http://fedworld.ntis.gov/index.html - Gateway to government information

Open Government Initiative - http://www.whitehouse.gov/open

Freedom of Information Act (FOIA) – http://www.foia.gov

Presidential Directives and Where To Find Them - http://www.loc.gov/rr/news/directives.html

U.S. Budget - http://www.whitehouse.gov/omb/budget

U.S. Presidential Directives and Executive Orders
http://www.library.yale.edu/govdocs/presexec.html

White House Official Web site - http://www.whitehouse.gov

Federal Depository Library Program

Catalog of U.S. Government Publications - http://catalog.gpo.gov -
Provides an index of legacy print and online items, and of nearby federal depository libraries

Core Documents of Democracy - http://www.gpoaccess.gov/coredocs.html -
Provides direct online access to basic federal government documents

Federal Depository Library Program (FDLP) Directory - http://catalog.gpo.gov/fdlpdir/FDLPdir.jsp -
The FDLP Directory is searchable by state or area code, and is updated monthly.

Federal Digital System (FDsys) - http://www.gpo.gov/fdsys - Search or browse government documents and publications, and access metadata for these resources

Federal Register - https://www.federalregister.gov - The official record of Congress

MetaLib - http://metalib.gpo.gov - A GPO federated search engine for searching multiple U.S. federal government databases

FEDLINK

Federal Library Resources – http://www.loc.gov/flicc/resources/index_resources.html - Information and services developed by FEDLINK and its members

FEDLINK New Librarians Working Group Email List - http://www.loc.gov/flicc/about/FLICC_WGs/newfeds.html - This new group includes great information and networking opportunities for new federal library professionals.

Interlibrary Loan

OCLC http://www.oclc.org/en-US/services/resource-sharing.html

DOCLINE - http://www.nlm.nih.gov/docline - National Library of Medicine's automated interlibrary loan (ILL) request routing and referral system

ALA Form - Fact Sheet - http://www.ala.org/tools/libfactsheets/alalibraryfactsheet08

Intelligence Resources

Intelligence.gov - http://www.intelligence.gov - General information about the Intelligence Community (IC) and links to the 17 member agencies

Office of the Director of National Intelligence - http://www.dni.gov/index.php

National Strategy for Counterterrorism -   http://www.whitehouse.gov/sites/default/files/counterterrorism_strategy.pdf

National Geospatial-Intelligence Agency - https://www1.nga.mil

Judicial Branch

Federal Judiciary Home Page - http://www.uscourts.gov

Legislative Branch

Congress.gov – http://www.congress.gov - This new mobile site includes a Congressional directory, House & Senate information, Committees/Reports, legislation, Guide to Law Online, Glossary of Legislative Terms, & even educational information such as the legislative process. Thomas.gov will be incorporated within Congress.gov

Congressional Research Service Reports – http://fpc.state.gov/c18185.htm - Official and publicly released reports.

Laws and Regulations by Topic (USA.gov) - http://www.usa.gov/Topics/Reference-Shelf/Laws.shtml

Legal Information Institute (Cornell) - http://www.law.cornell.edu

Legislative Process Resources LibGuide - http://libguides.bgsu.edu/content.php?pid=9023&sid=58568 - Includes biographies, voting history, text of bills, floor votes, etc.

The Plum Book - http://www.gpo.gov/fdsys/pkg/GPO-PLUMBOOK-2012/content-detail.html - United

States Government Policy and Supporting Positions: 2012 Edition

U.S. Senate Virtual Reference Desk – http://www.senate.gov/pagelayout/reference/b_three_sections_with_teasers/virtual.htm

Management

All About Strategic Planning - http://managementhelp.org/strategicplanning - Provides a basic overview of strategic planning, but is not federal specific

American Management Association
http://www.amanet.org/
Training site with both onsite courses in all aspects of management in Washington DC and online courses

Competencies for Federal Librarians - http://www.loc.gov/flicc/publications/Lib_Compt/2011/2011Competencies.pdf

GS Graduate School Training & Professional Development
http://www.graduateschool.edu/
Training site with onsite and online courses in all aspects of Federal government including management

Handbook of Occupational Groups and Families - http://www.opm.gov/classapp/fedclass/gshbkocc.pdf - Position Classification Standards within Library & Archives Group

Hiring Reform - http://www.opm.gov/policy-data-oversight/human-capital-management/hiring-reform/#url=Hiring

Government Performance and Results Act (GPRA) Related Materials - http://www.whitehouse.gov/omb/mgmt-gpra/index-gpra

O*NET Online -
http://www.onetonline.org - Contracted by U.S. Department of Labor, detailed database of career skills and requirements with labor taxonomy

Performance.gov - http://www.performance.gov - Metrics and information about increasing government performance by streamlining processes, cutting back on waste, etc.

Personnel Assessment - http://apps.opm.gov/ADT/Content.aspx?page=home

U.S. Office of Government Ethics - http://www.oge.gov - Information regarding conflicts of interest, especially within the Executive Branch.

U.S. Office of Personnel Management - http://www.opm.gov

U.S. Office of Personnel Management (OPM) Handbooks http://www.opm.gov/ses/references/handbook.asp - Includes Guide to Senior Executive Service Qualifications

Maps and Plans

Library of Congress, Geography & Map Division (G&M) http://www.loc.gov/rr/geogmap Reading Room links including hours with more on our contemporary and historical (electronic and print) cartographic, geospatial, geographic, architectural, nautical maps/plans/charts/atlases along with reference services and even more educational information.

Federal Geospatial Data Center -
http://www.fgdc.gov - Federal interagency organization coordinates and disseminates federal geospatial data to maximize geospatial data efficacy and compatibility for optimal geospatial data analytics. The FGDC coordinates geospatial data such as recommended standards, guidelines, metadata, and even the new Geospatial Platform http://www. Geoplatform.gov/home/ --which can even be used to make Geographic Information System (GIS) maps.

Geographic Names Information System -
http://nhd.usgs.gov/gnis.html - Official US Government domestic and foreign location names, as required by federal agencies.   Incorporating these names within geographical data will maximize interoperability and streamline geospatial data analytics. This usage of Geographic Information System (GIS) data is especially relevant if the original data comes from federal resources--such as the US Census Bureau, the Central Intelligence Agency, or the National Geospatial-Intelligence Agency.

Map and Geospatial Information Round Table (MAGIRT) -
http://www.ala.org/magirt/sites/ala.org.magirt/files/content/publicationsab/VGI%20MAGIRT%20 EP%2012-postfinal.pdf - Just one of the MAGIRT resources with recent Volunteered Geographic Information (VGI) or crowd-sourcing resources, Spatial Data Infrastructures, open-sourced map creation, and other academic Geographic Information System (GIS) mapping resources.

Medical Resources

BioMed Central - http://www.biomedcentral.com - Provides access to 220 scientific, technical & medical open access journals

Centers for Disease Control and Prevention (CDC) - http://www.cdc.gov

National Center for Biotechnology Information (NCBI) - http://www.ncbi.nlm.nih.gov/guide

National Library of Medicine - http://www.nlm.nih.gov – This most useful resource includes ClinicalTrials.gov, medical terms, Human Genome Resources, Biomedical Research and Informatics, Toxnet, and more

Partners in Information Access for the Public Health Workforce - http://phpartners.org

PubMed - http://www.ncbi.nlm.nih.gov/pubmed - Includes more than 21 million citations for biomedical literature from MEDLINE, life science journals and online books

PubMed Central (PMC) - http://www.ncbi.nlm.nih.gov/pmc -
Provides full-text access to biomedical and life sciences journal literature at the National Institute for Health's National Library of Medicine (NIH/NLM)

Military Resources

ABCs of Military Resources – http://www.dtic.mil/dtic/annualconf/2010/ABCsMilitaryResources.pdf

Defense Technical Information Center (DTIC) – http://www.dtic.mil – Scientific, technical, engineering, and business related information – Federal government employees may register for access-controlled resources

Defense Sites for Searchers - http://www.dtic.mil/dtic/annualconf/2010/DefSitesforSearchers.pdf

DoD 101 – http://www.defense.gov/about/dod101.aspx - Introductory overview of the Defense Department

DoD Dictionary – http://www.dtic.mil/doctrine/dod_dictionary

Military Legal Resources – http://www.loc.gov/rr/frd/Military_Law/military-legal-resources-home. html

Military Publishing

Army Publishing – http://www.apd.army.mil
Air Force Publishing – http://www.e-publishing.af.mil
Defense Standards and Specifications - http://quicksearch.dla.mil
DoD Forms - http://www.dtic.mil/whs/directives/infomgt/forms
DoD Issuances – http://www.dtic.mil/whs/directives
DoD Publications – http://www.defense.gov/pubs
Joint Chiefs of Staff - http://www.dtic.mil/cjcs_directives
Marine Corps Publications - http://www.marines.mil/News/Publications.aspx
Navy Issuances – http://doni.daps.dla.mil/default.aspx

Professional Organizations

American Association of Law Libraries (AALL) - http://www.aallnet.org

Federal Law Librarians Caucus - http://www.aallnet.org/caucus/fllc

Government Documents Special Interest Group (GD-SIS) - http://www.aallnet.org/sections/gd

American Library Association (ALA) - http://www.ala.org

Federal and Armed Forces Libraries Round Table (FAFLRT) - http://www.ala.org/ala/mgrps/rts/faflrt

Government Documents Round Table (GODORT) - http://www.ala.org/ala/mgrps/rts/godort

Professional Tips Wiki -http://wikis.ala.org/professionaltips/index.php?title=Main_Page#Welcome_to_the_ALA_Professional_Tips_Wiki

American Society for Information Sciences and Technology (ASIS&T) - http://www.asis.org

American Records Management Association (ARMA) - http://www.arma.org - Records creation, scheduling & disposition

FEDLIB - http://www.loc.gov/flicc/listsrvs.html - Federal librarians discussion list, a community of practice with training and some employment opportunities

Medical Library Association (MLA) - http://www.mlanet.org

Federal Libraries Section - http://fls.mlanet.org

Special Libraries Association (SLA) - http://www.sla.org

Government Information Division (DGI) - http://govinfo.sla.org

Military Libraries Division (DMIL) - http://military.sla.org

Solo Librarians Division - http://solo.sla.org

National Federation of Advanced Information Services (NFAIS) - http://www.nfais.org

Society of American Archivists (SAA) - http://www2.archivists.org

Government Records Section - http://www.archivists.org/saagroups/gov/index.asp

Lone Arrangers Roundtable - http://www2.archivists.org/groups/lone-arrangers-roundtable - log-in required.

Military Archives Roundtable - http://www2.archivists.org/groups/military-archives-roundtable - log-in required.

Professional Reading and Discussion Lists

- ψ Federal Computer Week
- ψ Government Computer News
- ψ NextGov
- ψ Federal News Radio
- ψ FEDLIB, Federal Library Discussion list from Library of Congress
- ψ Federal Employees Almanac (your library may have a copy)

Scientific and Technical Information

DTIC Online - http://www.dtic.mil

CENDI - http://www.cendi.gov - Interagency working group of senior scientific and technical information (STI) managers from 13 federal agencies producing federal information products –

GreyNet International - http://www.greynet.org

National Technical Information Service – http://www.ntis.gov - Technical reports, standards, etc.

Open Grey Literature Search - http://www.opengrey.eu

Science.gov – http://www.science.gov - Also available in Spanish.

Scientific Data Management (SDM) for Government Agencies - Harnessing the Power of Digital Data: Taking the Next Step – http://cendi.dtic.mil/publications/pub_CENDI-2011-1.pdf

WorldWideScience.org - http://worldwidescience.org
Standards and Best Practices

Academic Library Standards - http://www.ala.org/acrl/standards

Best Practices for Government Libraries - http://www.lexisnexis.com/legalnewsroom/litigation/b/litigation-blog/archive/2012/10/05/2012-best-practices-for-government-libraries-released.aspx - Released annually, and consisting of many articles written by federal librarians for federal librarians.

Cataloging tools - http://www.loc.gov/cds - Cataloging Distribution services and products -

Federal Records Management Responsibilities - http://www.archives.gov/records-mgmt

Library of Congress Authorities - http://authorities.loc.gov/cgi-bin/Pwebrecon.cgi?DB=local&PAGE=First - Searchable authority file of established name, title, subject, and keyword data authorities – useful for historical variants.

Library of Congress Standards - http://www.loc.gov/standards - Resource Description Formats, Digital Library Standards, Information Resource Retrieval Protocols, and more

Virtual International Authority File (VIAF) - http://www.viaf.org - Multilingual names from national libraries, archives, and museums, published by OCLC.

Z39.50 - http://www.loc.gov/z3950 - Gateway to Library Catalogs

Statistics and Datasets American Fact Finder – http://factfinder2.census.gov/faces/nav/jsf/pages/index.xhtml - Search facts from U.S. Census Bureau surveys

Data.gov - http://www.data.gov - Provides descriptions, information about access, and tools for using Federal government datasets

DMDC Data Request System (DRS) - https://www.dmdc.osd.mil/dmdcrs/ - A service available to federal employees for obtaining statistical information on personnel, manpower, training and financial data in the Department of Defense

FEDSTATS – http://www.fedstats.gov - Statistics from more than 70 U.S. Federal agencies -

Geo.data.gov – http://geo.data.gov

GovPulse - http://govpulse.us - A mobile-friendly, interactive site making the Federal Register more searchable and accessible to the public.

Organization for Economic Co-operation and Development (OECD)
Statistics - http://www.oecd.org/statistics

Technology Architect's Virtual Capitol - http://www.capitol.gov

Connecting with the Library of Congress - http://www.loc.gov/homepage/connect.html

DataMasher - http://www.datamasher.org - Create mash-ups with state data

E-Government - http://www.state.gov/r/pa/wm/egov/index.htm - Includes mobile technology information, such as device-agnostic design

Government Ethics and the Use of Social Media - Social media ethics information, including privacy, impartiality, and security. http://www.fcc.gov/maps

HowTo.gov - http://www.howto.gov - Helping government workers deliver a better customer experience to citizens

Info.apps.gov - Information on cloud computing for the federal community

Issuemap.org - http://www.issuemap.org - Create maps with Excel & CSD or CSV files, a project from the Federal Communications Commission (FCC)

Mobile Technology - http://mobilegovwiki.howto.gov/home - Mobile.gov wiki

National Archives (NARA) - http://www.archives.gov/research/search - Social tagging enabled OPAC

National Library of Medicine http://pubmedhh.nlm.nih.gov (without navigation go.usa.gov/xFb)

Office of E-Government and Information Technology - http://www.whitehouse.gov/omb/e-gov

Official US Government Web Portal - http://www.usa.gov

Official US Government Search Engine - http://search.usa.gov

Smithsonian Institution - http://www.si.edu/apps/smithsonianmobile

There's a Congressional App for That - http://blogs.loc.gov/law/2011/06/theres-a-congressional-app-for-that - Congress, apps & tour of Congress

LIBRARY OF
CONGRESS
FEDLINK

Federal Library and Information Network

101 Independence Ave, SE ~ Washington, DC 20540-4935

FEDLINK Main Number ~ (202) 707-4800

FEDLINK Hotline ~ (202) 707-4900

www.ingramcontent.com/pod-product-compliance
Lightning Source LLC
Chambersburg PA
CBHW080443290526
45791CB00008BA/2593